T0062884

HARD leads to SOFT
or
SOFT leads to HARD

HARD leads to SOFT
or
SOFT leads to HARD

Decoding Industrial Relations for
Business-People Synergy

Dr K. Suresh Kumar

PARTRIDGE

To order additional copies of this book, contact
Partridge India
000 800 10062 62
orders.india@partridgepublishing.com

www.partridgepublishing.com/india

Contents

Dedication

Dedicated to my caring, departed mother, Saroja. But for her irresistible concern for my academic well-being, I would be nothing in my professional career.

'The inspiration you provided me will remain tallest throughout my life.'

~ Dr K. Suresh Kumar

Foreword

Human beings are complex and unpredictable in some ways. Past theories and insights help us predict to some extent and in certain situations. In complex cultures like India, predictability becomes difficult as many variables are at work. In Human Resources Management, while there may be principles and values, there is not one way of dealing with any given issue. Those at the bottom of the organisational ladder are the real contributors to organisational performance. Human Resources Management deals with competency building, commitment building, and culture building. HR systems deal with providing peace, stability, and growth. Like in Maslow's need hierarchy theory, HR Management theory outlines 'peace' as an essential prerequisite for organisational performance. This fulfils the basic needs of an organisation. HR managers through appropriate Industrial Relations interventions create such peace. A good IR climate is necessary to ensure peace.

Dr K. Suresh Kumar, an accomplished HR professional with more than two decades of experience on managing Industrial Relations situation with Employee Relations perspectives, has provided through this book a lot of insights both relevant to theory and practice.

It is widely said that the behaviour of Trade Unions or their representatives at the table of negotiations and decision making is more often manifestation of management philosophy as well as policies in guiding industrial relations. This real-time case documented by the Dr Suresh Kumar brings out basic nuances apart from strategic dimensions in managing Trade Union relations for lasting peace.

The case demonstrates amply that good Employee Relations can be built through positive outlook, collaborative values, and proactive management strategy. In dealing with people in an organisation trust, mutuality and empathy are essential ingredients that build good Employee Relations. They form the intellectual capital of the organisation and get manifested through motivated, supportive, and proactive unions and workmen. This emphasis is what distinguishes this book from others.

Over a period of time, HR has been over-focusing on HR as Strategic Business partner and as a result the significance of PEOPLE as the cause and consequence of business has gone to the background. This book clearly highlights vignettes of People dimension of Business Management and particularly in dealing with Industrial Relations situations. The episodes involving Equitable Compensation, Employee Discipline, Legal Solutions respecting employee sentiments or Communication Strategies adopted or for that matter interface between internal or External Union relationships, etc., all narrates the imperative of having a very positive and at times neutral approach in solving complex Industrial Relations issues.

Sometimes a tough stand taken by the HR in dealing with stalemate underscores the importance of HR role in protecting business interests. The aftermath of these decisions and its unconditional acceptance by both internal and external stakeholders corroborates this fine balancing act on the part of Human Resources, as indicated in this case study. This real-time case study vividly exposes the value of Leadership Integrity towards long-term industrial peace.

I am sure this attempt of the author Dr K. Suresh Kumar will surely benefit the management and HR diaspora through transfer of experience in the form of documented knowledge management text. This will provide not only knowledge but wisdom partnership for budding HR professionals and management students. Employee Relations aspect of Human Resources needs to be experienced more than acquired through theoretical lessons.

Documenting real-time experiences by management practitioners is always a commendable contribution to the development of profession and professional practice. This becomes even more appreciable when it deals with Human Resources Management issues. I congratulate Dr Suresh Kumar for taking pains to document his experiences and approaches and make the results available for wider readership. I wish this book great success with all managers, management students, CEOs, teachers, students, and particularly HR professionals.

Dr T. V. Rao
Chairman, TVRLS, and former professor at
IIMA and L&T professor of HRD at XLRI.

Preface

Motivation for this book: Undaunted Conviction

People often ask, 'What prompts me to undertake this challenging literary project?' An absolutely sensible question. The answer is 'Conviction' and 'Transfer of Experience'. A conviction that truthful HR leadership would turn any challenging Industrial Relations into a great Business Opportunity through effective mutual communication and positive relationship with workforce. Secondly, Industrial Relations is an area of Human Resources Management that per se cannot be learnt through cognitive process but it is only through experiential sharing/learning that the art and science of Industrial Relations might well be understood.

HARD leads to SOFT or SOFT leads to HARD

There is no right or wrong approach in dealing with existing or emerging industrial relations challenges that normally occur in organisations. It's no more denying the fact that any approach, which HR resorts to, must result into long-term harmony and business advantage. In other words, IR decisions must culminate into positive consequences. Implied in the above sentence is that some of IR decisions' efficacy might be known immediately, whilst for some others, the consequences may justify the righteousness or otherwise of IR decision. For easy understanding, IR approaches are revivified as HARD and SOFT approaches. As the names resonate, HARD stands for Assertive/

informed decisions, no-holds barred approaches to manage a given situation, role-based decisions to amplify one's prerogative, aggressive or strong reaction or decision and its execution thereof or it can be a reactive approach to SOFT decisions. SOFT approach stands for supportive decisions, facilitative reaction, empathetic response, or well-conceived decisions keeping in mind certain expected outcomes or it can be a reactive approach to HARD decisions. Or, even it could be a judicious mix of both HARD and SOFT approaches. Depending on the various situations, either of the approaches or a combination of both can be resorted to by the management and union/employees to achieve their respective goals.

LIVE CASE STUDY

HARD leads to SOFT or SOFT leads to HARD is a live case study on Industrial Relations (implies suspension of operations and reopening of the plant operations) involving application and interpretation of relevant provisions of labour acts, conciliation machinery, adjudication, management of Internal and external union leadership, management of a plant during a crisis situation, dealing with political and government functionaries, management of law enforcement machinery and fourth estate, dealing with socio-psychological and familial aspects of employees, overall issues in dealing with operations/line management, and finally effectiveness of HR to act as spokesman between top management (promoters) and those managed.

1) At the end of every chapter or relevant episode (being described), the Title Lineage is explained with required amplification to provide practical insights by focusing on the consequences experienced.

2) Industrial Relations and Business Interface is explained in the light of the need for planning and execution of various Industrial Relations Strategies to be adopted to manage the situations.

3) How the given Industrial Relations scenarios could be managed towards long-term harmony and peace leading to Employee Relations.

All the three facets mentioned above shall surely provide application skills or awareness of certain techniques apart from applied knowledge in managing industrial relations towards harmonious Employee Relations keeping in mind both workforce and business dimensions. As such, this literary work on *live* Industrial Relations *episodes* with Business Connect and People Connect is expected to fill the vacuum to certain extent in taking crucial decisions in managing industrial conflicts towards long-term Employee Relations, both for emerging/budding management and HR professionals apart from serving the reference book purpose for other stakeholders in the learning vector such as consultants and practicing management professionals.

Industrial Relations to Employee Relations

With the emergence of GenX workforce coupled with business complexities which forces the management to adopt newer forms of staffing (contract and temp engagement), conventional Employee Relations issues such as grievances, fair treatment, opportunities for career growth, nonemployment challenges, work-life balancing, etc., are getting re-enacted. Here HR needs to strengthen the workplace relationship through various engagement programs apart from supporting the workforce with equitable economic and social benefits. Employee Relations

(ER) envisages preventive approach to industrial conflicts whereas Industrial Relations (IR) provides strategies/processes to manage the same. ER is a very proactive and long-term focused structured approach which presupposes trust and collaborations with people towards business development.

Here every attempt is being made to explain how the paradigm shift can be brought in by focusing on integrity, trust building, and nonpolitical transparent approach in dealing with unions/employees in the backdrop of various situations. This book also explains the consequences of this approach in providing a long-term solution to industrial peace and business excellence. Business excellence here implies 'How Industrial Engineering approach could become a handy tool for HR in establishing a work culture based on accountability and measurement of productivity/quality'. This is nothing but the exposition of untold dimension of Industrial Engineering as branch of Management Science towards Employee Relations.

Structure of this book

The whole book is structured in such a manner that readers would be able to start and conclude their learning process in a flow process manner. The relevant exhibits or illustrations are provided in a continuum to assist the readers in connecting the dots very easily. The whole real-time case experience is divided into eight parts:

Part 1 deals with introduction about the business group and the company, its products, competitive kaleidoscope, and the overall Industrial Relations situation.

Part 2 describes Industrial Relations episodes or events which turned out to be the source of learning for both management and unions. Also, it deals with evolving situations and how the management and unions strategised their plan of action and moved ahead.

Part 3 covers communication strategies adopted by the management in dealing with internal and external stakeholders. How this was being viewed and reaction from the union are also being capitulated.

Part 4 focuses on negotiation strategies initiated by the management in spite of legal imbroglio and the reaction of Trade Union/its members. In addition, this part takes the readers through the balancing act to be performed by the management between discipline and welfare, and how difficult it is for the management to run the business if the Industrial Relations situation turns to be hostile.

Part 5 provides deep insights into the interface between the business and Human Resources with special reference to Industrial Relations domain. Effectiveness of Industrial Relations to a true extent relies upon its connect with the business and people dimensions. Here ample explanation is given on how HR professionals must be mindful of both long-term and short-term Industrial Relations measures and its consequences on business and people aspects. This part also heralds the bipartite process and its genesis apart from the events which really facilitated the reopening of the plant post hostilities. Very significant part of this content is devoted for explaining Performance Linked Pay based on scientific study of Productivity Indices.

Part 6 takes the learning fraternity through last-minute developments which put certain hurdles in the joint endeavour of management and union to conclude the 12(3) settlement. It also explains, with certain solid research backup, how the management and the union can cocreate an ecosystem through sustainable long-term industrial peace.

Part 7 focuses on the structure and template of 12(3) settlement reached between the management and the Trade Union.

Part 8 covers concluding remarks on the part of the author based on several research findings and discussions with senior HR professionals on the imperatives of paradigm shift from Industrial Relations to Employee Relations. Apart from the 'WHY' part, the 'HOW' part is also covered.

It is to be submitted that title connect (the title of this book HARD leads to SOFT or SOFT leads to HARD and its relationship with various Industrial Relations episodes captured in this book work) is editorialised by the author at the relevant points in all the chapters of this book. Plus, the epithet 'HR & business interface' takeaways in the context of various Industrial Relations situations and their impact/consequences are also scripted at the appropriate spaces. The esteemed readers of this book may find this humble attempt very useful in their professional realm.

Acknowledgements

This book is born out of a real-time experience of Industrial Relations in a manufacturing plant encountered by the author directly, having immense pedagogical value both in professional management and academic spaces. My initial years of professional experience in Human Resources and Industrial Relations coupled with own academic penchant helped to resolve the dispute in an amicable manner by putting an ecliptic perspective such as Business Sustenance, People Welfare, and Employee Relations in one silo and manage the situation. This coupled with HR leadership integrity shall transform any Industrial Relations situations into Employee Relations resulting in permanent industrial harmony.

I must thank, with copious gratitude, all Leadership Team, Trade Union Team, and external stakeholders for having given such a wonderful opportunity to get involved into the finer nuances of the issues providing a way forward to resolve the stalemate, which provided a great concrete platform for me to share the learning with management and Academic Diaspora.

My constant inspiration to document my professional experiences is Prof TSN Pillai, formerly of Loyola School of Management, Trivandrum. I pay rich tribute to him.

I take this opportunity to remember, with tons of gratitude, Mr AS Girish, Head HR Apollo Tyres (Kerala Manufacturing cluster), who for the first time identified HR talents in me and initiated me into the HR profession.

It is my proud privilege to have this book endorsed by none other than Prof Dave Ulrich and Prof Wayne Brockbank of University of Michigan's Ross School of Business. I consider this as a great honour for my humble attempt.

I owe thanks to Dr TV Rao, former HRM professor, Indian Institute of Management Ahmedabad, and a widely acclaimed global HR guru for having written a wonderful foreword encompassing the salient features of this book and how this is going to benefit all stakeholders of business and management, particularly a leap forward focus to HR professionals.

I am really fortunate to get pre-publishing editing support from Mrs Indu Madhavi Iragavarapu and my colleague Ghantasala Bhasker who stood with me throughout this process. Additionally, they also provided the much needed professional support in organising the contents into a meaningful format. Special thanks for their editorial assistance.

I must also thank Kathey Lorenzo, Publishing and Editing Associate of Partridge Publishing, for her consistent efforts and commitment to fine tune this script to the highest level of accuracy.

Most significantly, a great kudos to my spouse, Sangeetha, who really tolerated my writing obsession.

Dr K. Suresh Kumar

Introduction

Are management fraternity or HR diaspora endowed with rich end to end script based on live Industrial Relations experiences? Assuming that if scripts are available, do they provide not only the knowledge but tacit understanding and vital decisional inputs to the genuine stakeholders? Is there any set of quick-fix wonder formula being made available to fix composite nature of Industrial Relations issue? What is the right HR leadership approach or style that is being called for to find permanent solution to the simmering IR challenges being surfaced in various industrial or service sectors? Is there any alternative model of Industrial Relations to the predominantly pursued reactionary model for short-term solutions? Has the time come to answer cohesively Peter F Drucker's time-tested adage: HR needs to finance union for its existence?

I remember the main body and contents of the NYT bestseller 'What they don't teach you at Harvard Business School' by Mark H McCormack. You have to depend on your wisdom to find definitive answers based on your own experience and exposure, coupled with your sense of leadership values to support the business and the people in an authenticated manner. Each Industrial Relations situation is unique to itself and there is no quick-fix solution that can be copied from any sources or leadership development programs or virtual chat through Social Media or from the tacit or un-tacit world of knowledge from WWW. Here much more than competency or experience, your overall perspective and leadership values drive the Industrial Relations situation to a logical conclusion being acceptable to all stakeholders.

Not as a pioneer, but rather a student being exposed to different Industrial Relations scenarios in various sectors (single to multiple union scenarios and business situations) have really taught me one basic tenet of managing Industrial Relations, i.e. 'be truthful to yourself'. It is easier to manage unions or shop floor workers through their affiliations than managing vertical/horizontal leadership in organisations. The model of Industrial Relations leadership based on Leadership Integrity can be considered as 'Centre of Gravity' for me to document this live Industrial Relations experience.

This can bring paradigm shift from Industrial Relations to trusteeship model of Employee Relations for lasting industrial harmony. This really has been the inspiration for this book.

Confidentiality

The author has got express permission from the top leadership of the company to share the experience for professional knowledge repository and supplementing the same as a contributory endeavour to the world of Business Management. As such, all aspects governing the company and its line of Business Management including identity of union and state and state government or other actors are kept anonymous.

Pattern of reading this book

As mentioned in the preface, this a documentary case study on a real-life Industrial Relations experiences which happened in a business unit having a single union employing close to 1,000 workforce. All eight parts of this book have been written in a sequential and structured manner. Therefore, to have a continuity and ease of understanding, esteemed readers are humbly suggested to go through these scribes in sequential manner. Nevertheless, all the ingredients are carefully added not to lose the continuum. Since it is presented in a storyboard writing style, it can be assimilated without getting into the bibliography or a directory of theories. Of course, the glossary of terms used are mentioned at the end of this book.

Feedback

I acknowledge with absolute gratitude any feedback:
drsureshhrm@gmail.com / drsureshhrm@yahoo.co.in

Basic architecture of learning derived from predominantly this documented case study on what really helped the management or HR to find an amicable solution to Industrial Relations standoff is outlined in the following epitaph:

Cursory dive into organisational challenges of the future

The organisational challenges of the future will no longer revolve around waging a war for talent or managing performance or developing people. While these will continue to remain important, the solutions for these will be plenty, and adequate competencies will evolve to address these needs. The challenges of the future will be in three distinct areas:

1. managing all the critical aspects of an organisation's relationship with its workforce;
2. helping organisations endure the onslaught of turbulence, structural changes, ownership changes, leadership changes and still remain committed to its larger purpose; and
3. building leadership competencies and governance systems.

Having underscored all challenges in three distinct areas, the differentiators in managing work force relations in corporations can broadly be summarised as below:

A. Proactive HR Leadership: As champion of productivity for business and champion of business continuity and economic benefits for Trade Unions.
B. Mass Leadership: How to contain, legitimately, the tendency of workforce to take leadership positions by overriding elected leadership. Recently, too, PENN ORUMAI (meaning, Women Power), a mass leadership union floated by plantation women labour force in Munnar (Kerala) by disregarding their affiliation to political union, is a pointer to reckon with.
C. Approach: Firm and fair approach in dealing with discipline and act as a spokesman in favour of workforce with the management.
D. Ensuring Acceptance: Ensure the acceptance of both government and bureaucracy. HR is expected to act as knowledge partners in their endeavour

to establish industrial harmony in the state. HR needs to be an expert fountain of knowledge on one hand and gain the goodwill on the other hand by maintaining professional image and connect with them on equal footing.

E. Keep the Door Open: Keep the door open for negotiation and communication with union and government functionaries. No strategy on less or no communication would any way help to overcome the hostilities unless it's a well-informed plan to put positive pressure on the union to adopt a constructive approach. Again proactive communication must be established with all important internal and external stakeholders, i.e., government functionaries, law and order authorities, if required, media as well.

F. Positive Pressure: Need to put positive pressure on the system and thereby exhaust all options including legal and political support with an objective to make the union people realise 'what is right and wrong' towards a permanent settlement of dispute rather than arrive at certain compromise for a short-term respite.

G. Principle-centred HR Leadership: Maintain the same level of communication with both Internal and External Union leadership in terms of both contour and context. If there is any inconsistency in the communication being opted by HR vis-à-vis External and Internal Union leadership, sooner than later HR will lose the stature of being a credible partner in the settlement process.

H. Courage to take timely decision: Begin with the end in mind. If the right sense of wisdom eludes union, irrespective of immaculate voices from both within and outside the union space, HR must be courageous enough to take quick action without being dragged by what is legally or morally right. Nevertheless, be informed of consequences of such decision and be prepared with necessary buffer solution to keep the situation from going out of control at any point in time.

I. Empower External and Internal Union leadership: Apportion credit to External Union leadership in gaining much needed acceptance from Internal Union team and to Internal Union leadership for not letting workmen lose confidence on them. HR leadership would get umpteen opportunities to discharge this role either before, during, or post hostility periods.

J. Avoid direct actions with wider ramifications: HR should avoid certain direct action that may have far reaching maim on the psyche of workmen. Remember the adage that 'nothing may infuse irreparable damage to the psychology of people'. As far as possible, HR or business leadership must desist from enjoying pyrrhic victory. Rather, business must aim at conclusive absolute win-win solution in dealing with union management issues. Intimidating the workmen by physical coercion, detention via law and order agencies, inflicts a deep-rooted psychological damage which may take long periods of time to get erased. Both of them need to join their hands to work together in the days to come, and knowingly or unknowingly, HR should not drag the situation to an uncontrollable level in dealing with IR issues at stake.

K. Line management support: Transition from Industrial Relations to Employee Relations presupposes the existence of strong line management–HR relationship and communication. In operational terms, HR would be instrumental in connecting with and soliciting their support, in terms of their role, in creating common understanding among the rank-and-file. One underpinning is that line management team would like to get involved in union management issues. There is a strong sense of psychological motivation for them to get engaged in particularly when operational issues are a galore due to IR situation. Considering their clout with shop floor team, HR should initiate constructive dialogue with line team with necessary caveat so that collaborative efforts yield intended fruits.

L. Professionally led union is a great force for improving management performance. It forces the manager to think about what he is doing and to be able to explain his actions and behaviour.

Background of the Case | 1

A BRIEF HISTORY OF THE BUSINESS GROUP

To know the occurrences of the incident, this took place at an Indian Metropolis. The organisation has been an ace in the business of production and distribution of glass containers. Founded in the early 1950s by a visionary entrepreneur, this is India's first fully automatic glass container manufacturing plant.

Manufacturing all varieties of glass bottles/vials, its facilities strategically encompass all the four provinces of East, North, West, and South of India for synergetic B2B approach. The south and east plants are expanded facilities with state-of-the-art induction furnace for manufacturing of castings in its own foundry. The group has incorporated its technology from the leaders of the Europe and USA. With a fully automated electronic inspection system, globally abreast quality control, and R&D, the organisation defines world class in all aspects.

ABOUT THE PLANT

It is a single-furnace plant with a melting capacity of 350 MT per day. The outstanding features of the plant are fully automated batch mixing facility with four lines of glass making IS machines. On-site printing, with three decoration lines and on-line automatic OI inspection machines, the rarest of its kind in the country, make it stand out in the milieu, which is further augmented by Sand Beneficiation plant, Foundry and Mould workshop.

The company's workforce is around 240 to 250 management staff and about 300 contract labour force. At any given point in time, the employee strength would vary anywhere between 720 and 800. The plant's turnover was approximately 110 crores in the year 2004–2005.

PREVAILING IR SITUATION

The company was under US-based business conglomerate until February 2002, later acquired by a business group in the year March 2002. A general myth that US-based groups are not really focused on labour–management relationship became a primary factor for the union to gain an edge over the management. Contrary to multinational style of management, the new management was assertive and worked on a mutual give-and-take model. To adduce a point in this aspect, new dispensation made the union agree on the extension of last bilateral agreement for another year from July 2004. Some of the main reasons for this being escalation of raw material cost, poor price realisation, cheap import of glass containers from China, and replacement of glass bottles by nonglass packaging.

Extension of Settlement: A Bipartite Discussion

Due to the economic-, commerce-, business-, and labour-related reasons, the previous owner of this company had to divest this plant to the well-known corporate business group in March 2002. The agreement signed by the old management and the union expired on 30 June 2004. Subsequently, bipartite discussion took place between management and union and it was agreed to extend the said agreement up to 30 June 2005. The reason for the agreement being the precarious financial condition of the company and on account of rebuilding the furnace with the additional capital investment of Rs.50 crores with an interest burden to the tune of Rs.7 crores per annum. Furnace rebuilding was necessitated to improve the quality of glass containers apart from productivity- and safety-related aspects.

In response to the Memorandum of Demands submitted by the union, the management served a notice on change of working conditions under section 9A of Industrial Disputes Act, 1947. Among other things, 9A notice sought to remove canteen and transportation subsidy, provision of leave as per the relevant statutes, etc.

Meanwhile, the union gave a notice of strike opposing the management's move to introduce changes under 9A provisions of ID Act without really coming to the negotiation table with explicit Charter of Expectation for bilateral settlement, which was long overdue.

The conciliation machinery, which seized of the dispute involving the union and the management, had convened several rounds of bilateral discussion to arrive at a settlement between the disputants but to no avail.

The union contention was on the following premise:

- Instead of submitting Charter of Expectations, the management was trying to hoodwink the workers by offering benefits out of reduction of privileges already enjoyed by the people in the guise of 9A provision under Industrial Disputes Act.
- The union and workmen were sensitive to the competitive situation of the glass industry and hence allowed the management to extend the agreement for one more year from July 2003. This was a gesture of goodwill to the new management for running the industry in a viable manner.

The management contention was on the following premise:

- The furnace rebuild, at the cost of 85 crores (capital plus five months interest), was undertaken not only for the long-term survival of the company but also keeping in mind the best interest of the employees.
- 9A Notice was issued with a purpose to implement certain provisions to improve operational viability and stability of the company on long-term basis. It was unfortunate to observe that instead of taking constructive stand on the implementation of 9A provisions, the union preferred a strike notice.

Troubled IR Situation When the Conciliation is Under Progress

As the normal situation was soon getting out of control, because of intimidating and muscle-flexing approach on the part of the union, the management found it appropriate to keep the government informed of the prevailing IR climate in the factory. To have a broad picture of the ground realities, the gist of the letter sent to appropriate government authority is reproduced below:

Exhibit #1

INDUSTRIAL RELATIONS SITUATION REPORT

This is to bring to the notice of all concerned that during the pendency of conciliation proceedings before the Conciliation Officer, any direct action on the part of Trade Union to alter the working conditions is unjustified and hence cannot be legally acceptable.

You all know that next conciliation meeting is scheduled to be conducted soon. But unfortunately, union in the company has resorted to unfair labour practices in the following manner.

- *Vitiating the mutual climate for bipartite negotiation by black flag protest.*
- *Brazenly instigating the workmen to refuse overtime.*
- *Indulging in other unfair practice of gathering workmen in the company premises for striking the assigned works.*

It is to be noted that the management has not closed the channels of bipartite discussion with union. But unfortunately, the workmen started refusing overtime (OT) causing irreparable damages to the plant and machinery besides production loss. This is absolutely unwarranted especially when the conciliation is in progress.

Once again we would like to reiterate that instigating people to strike work including refusal of OT shall cause irreparable damages to the continuous process industry like ours. Disruption in the continuous process industry like ours may cause catastrophical effect in the form of furnace damage leading to the loss of production and equipment damage.

Under this difficult situation, the management does not have any other option other than taking drastic measures including the closure of unit for which the union and its members shall be squarely held responsible.

It is a preferred course of action on the part of management to keep the appropriate govt informed of occurrences and IR related events at regular intervals. In the process, appropriate govt. authority may take cognizance of the matter and initiate fair course of action to deal with the situation.

- Exhibit Ends -

FAILURE OF CONCILIATION

From the inception of the conciliation meeting, the Labour Officer (Conciliation) advised the union to submit their objections in written statement, though they agreed, they failed to file their written reply despite several opportunities given. Hence final hearing was posted based on the consensual date and time. During the final hearing, the union again sought adjournment since their honourable president was not available and did not file their written reply. The workmen orally refused to accept the changes, whereas the management wanted the changes to be strictly implemented without any violations.

The conciliation officer has taken all possible measures to bring about amicable settlement of dispute. Since the parties were found to be adamant vis-à-vis their positions, conciliation officer had no other go but to prefer a failure report.

> *CAPTION LINEAGE: Very assertive stand (HARD approach) which was taken by the management probably resulted into certain conclusion in terms of moving to the next stage of dispute resolution. How this would manifest in terms of settlement is to be seen . . .*

⚜

Turn of Events to the Consternation of Management | 2

Leveraging on time required for the appropriate government to notify further remedies under Industrial Disputes Act for final resolution of 9A disputes, the management was pondering over implementation of purported changes. Like a bolt from the blue, the union succeeded in getting Interim Injunction from High Court restraining the management in implementing 9A changes. An environment characterised by dynamic Industrial Relations situation, mutual resolution of difference of opinion, or disputes seems to be more finite form of settlement rather than time-consuming legal remedy and thereby prompting disputants in hostile camps.

What Has Gone Wrong for the Management?

All through the course of conciliation, Senior Management of the company used to apprise HODs/Section Heads about the progress of the discussion with the union. Like solipsist's attitude, Senior Management had voiced Big Brother's right by telling the team that it is determined to implement 9A without realising the fact that interaction dynamics with union colleagues who work with shop floor would come in touch with managerial 'Come whatever be' stand which might embolden the union to go to any extent to wriggle out of the crisis situation. Equally, the union also finds it absolutely essential to keep its folks together through some defensive strategies without allowing the management to rein in them.

A Big Lesson for the Management

Managing communication was observed to be an area of concern especially when IR situation is disturbed. The management did not realise the shop floor dynamics wherein HODs and union representatives/workmen share their opinion and feelings. Perhaps, seepage of information through the management staff on purported action contemplated by the management could have triggered aggressive response on the part of the union.

> *CAPTION LINEAGE:* No compromise on what the management intends to do (HARD approach) resulted into an unprecedented reaction from the union. Probably HARD stand had to be taken but we need not allow this hard strategy to be shared with anyone in the given situation.

Turn of events were not conducive for *Healthy Industrial Relations*

The union succeeded in getting injunction order from High Court that restrained the management from implementing 9A changes. The management had no premonition that this would happen. This created a schism between the parties making the situations worse and non-conducive for a smooth signing of the settlement.

- Senior Management/leadership did not make any effort for the resumption of bilateral discussion.
- The union on the other hand had to contend with irresistible pressure within the cadre for speedy resumption of bilateral talks with the management.
- The union started showing their anger and displeasure by organising gate meetings and slogan shouting.
- Observed 'Black Day' by wearing black badges.

MANAGEMENT'S JUSTIFICATION FOR ITS RELUCTANCE TO RESUME TALKS

One of the major provisions of 9A notice given by the management was the continuity of prevailing 12(3) settlement earlier signed. Since the implementation of 9A notice per se was restrained by the High Court, the management could not resume bilateral negotiation as the matter is sub judice. Though the management's stand is legally justified, but in providing a healthy stimulus to the ongoing turbulence in IR situation, there could be different view in IR. Reaching out to the Bargaining Zone wherein one finds that its ultimate objectives would be realised, is a process tactic normally adopted by the parties to the dispute.

> **CAPTION LINEAGE:** *Tactical negotiation stand (HARD approach) had proven to be either unanticipated or intolerable for the union. HARD stand had started yielding SOFT response from the union. Again, SOFT response could be seen as an outcome of HARD experiences the union might have undergone.*

LESSONS FOR THE UNION:

It was a far imagination element for the union to understand that the management can reject union overtures for a bilateral discussion adhering to sub judice principle.

PRECARIOUSLY PERCHED

The management's insistence on the union to withdraw their writ petition in the High Court for the resumption of bilateral negotiation coupled with lumpen elements' exertion of pressure on the union leadership made it untenable for the union except to go for a confrontation mode in dealing with the management. Incidents of overtime refusal, slogan shouting, Go Slow, etc, were occurring at regular intervals.

CAPTION LINEAGE: The management's no-holds-barred (HARD) approach precipitated the union reaction in the form of a HARD one. Probably the union could have felt that Interim Injunction in favour of the union, restraining the management towards implementation of 9A changes, would SOFTEN the management response. Rather it proved to be counterproductive.

Communication Campaign by the Management | 3

Meanwhile, the management thought it prudent to communicate to the workmen at large about the actual business challenges, competitive reality being faced by the company, relevance of 9A notice, the management position, etc. It was perceived that the people would get a very clear download of these relevant aspects governing the union-management relationship

DETAILED NOTE ON
INDUSTRIAL RELATIONS CLIMATE

Exhibit #2

<u>LONG-TERM SETTLEMENT</u>

This is to bring to your kind attention that the last long-term settlement signed between the management and the union is expired on 30th June 2005. Subsequently, the management has initiated several measures including dialogue and discussion with the union and their members for the peaceful settlement of wage agreement.

Running business in this highly competitive period demands higher productivity, cost control and continuous quality improvement. Moreover ever changing customer demands call for frequent modification in the production design, systems, and technology, In addition to this, input costs are on the upward trend. In order to survive in this volatile business environment, it is necessary that trade union should unconditionally support the management initiatives to ensure the stability and growth of the plant operations.

Earlier option of increasing the price of products to make an industrial unit viable has been ruled out. The only way and the best way to ensure the profitability of concern is to cut down the cost wherever possible. Otherwise, the very survival of the company shall be in jeopardy affecting the lives of employees and their family members. This is very true in our case, too.

9A NOTICE:

The management has issued 9A Notice dated 5th July 2005 with a purpose to implement certain provisions so as to improve operational viability and stability of the company on long-term basis. It is observed that instead of taking constructive stand on the implementation of 9A provisions, the union has given a strike notice dated 6th July 2005 and subsequently the matter has been referred before the conciliation officer pending resolution.

BUSINESS REALITY

In anticipation of better business prospects, the company management has decided to go for furnace rebuilt in Sept '03 at a cost of approximately Rs.85 crores. But contrary to our expectation, the company faced massive setback in sales due to high competition and slump in the demand for certain product segment.

Glass industries all over India have been under severe crunch and instability due to the shortfall in demand and unprecedented threat from substituted products.

In this connection, we would like to bring to your kind attention the following real situation:

COMPANY NAME	**REAL SITUATION**
Glass Company A	*Stopped one production line on account of accumulated stock.*
Glass Company B	*Completely stopped two production lines and decided to close down one furnace.*
Glass Company C	*Instead of running full production lines they are now running only two lines due to substantial stock to be liquidated.*
Glass Company D	*Out of 5 furnaces, they have already closed down 3 furnaces.*
Glass Company E	*Our own group company has already closed 2 production lines due to the accumulated stock position. It is still in the process of closing more production lines.*
Glass Company F	*Already shut down one furnace and due to slump in the glass market the plant has been undergoing repairs and maintenance.*
Glass Company G	*Due to severe demand crisis, the plant had to shut down 2 furnaces.*

The Phenomenal escalation of price with respect to critical inputs has resulted in whopping additional financial commitment to the tune of 10 crores in 2004–2005 compared to its previous year. The following table illustrates the same:

Additional financial commitment— Raw material—Price increase (PMT) Period Sept '03 and July '05

RAW MATERIAL	SEP '03 PRICE	JUL-05	DIFFERENCE	%	AVG MLY CONS	ADDITIONAL COST
Calcite	1,849	2,030	181/–	10	330	59,730.00
Dolomite	1,371	1,452	81/–	6	280	22,680.00
Limestone	1,402	1,422	20/–	1.5	669	13,380.00
Feldspar	1,638	1,806	168/–	10	356	59,808.00
Cullet	2,762	3,087	325/–	12	2410	783,250.00
Sheet glass	2,138	2,567	429/–	20	350	150,150.00
Selenium	875	7,500	6,625/–	758	120	90,960.00
Soda ash	7,352	9,447	2,095/–	29	969	2,030,055.00
Furnace oil (KL) April '04 –July '05	9,270	15,278	6,008/–	65	885	5,317,080.00
Additional monthly cost escalation						8,527,093.00
Annual additional cost burden						10.23 crores

Cost inflation for inputs will be substantial henceforth and expected to continue during the coming years.

THE FALL OF SOFTDRINKS BUSINESS: *The investment of approximately Rs.11 crores on Applied Ceramic Labeling has proven to be a dead investment as the soft drink glass containers, which were supposed to have 40% of the total sales, are now less than 5%.*

THREAT OF GLOBALISATION: *The glass containers of Chinese origin are being dumped in South Asian countries at a price* *less than Rs.10,000/– pmt. Since the cost of production is well above Rs.10,000/– pmt, there is a likely chance that the glass containers will start incurring losses. Many glass plants across India stand testimony of these forms of global cutthroat competition and closed their units in spite of the best management strategies adopted by them.*

It is observed that over the past few months, the cost of production and sales realisation have been showing inverse relationship due to adverse market realities and escalating cost of input. The following table substantiates this trend.

Cost Vs Sales Realisation

Month	Cost of Production (PMT)	Sales Realisation (PMT
April '05	*10,923*	*12,453*
May '05	*11,348*	*12,101*
June '05	*11,782*	*11,862*
July '05	*12,038*	*11,795*
	10% increase	*6% decrease*

The above table makes it clear that cost of production has increased by 10% and sales realisation has decreased by 6%.

SALARY COMPARISON OF THE PLANT WITH OTHER UNITS IN THE SAME GROUP

Since our company is a 100% subsidiary unit, it cannot be viewed in isolation from other group companies in terms of salary structure of employees. After the latest settlement, salary structure of employees at other plants is 20–25%

lower than what is being paid at this plant. The salary structure of employees at other units after recent settlement is lower than our present salary structure.

CTC COMPARISON (MONTHLY)

	Unit 1	Unit 2	Unit 3	Unit 4	Unit 5
Highly skilled	11,256	6,150	8,213	6,250	9,250
Skilled	9,709	5,917	8,011	4,801	8,200
Semi-skilled	8,180	5,806	7,930	4,580	6,300

This is to be noted that the salary structure of all other plants is for thirty-tree production lines whereas this 25% increase in salary structure of workmen at our plant is only for four production lines.

ACQUISITION HISTORY

Due to the economic, commerce, business and labour-related reasons, the previous owner of this company had to divest this plant to a bigger conglomerate in March 2002. The agreement signed by the management and the union expired on 30th June 2004. Subsequently, bipartite discussion took place between the management and the union and it was agreed to extend the said agreement up to 30th June 2005. This agreement was reached on account of precarious financial condition of the company and on account of rebuilding of furnace with the additional capital investment of Rs.50/– crores and the servicing of interest burden to the tune of Rs.7 crores per annum. This itself is very sufficient to justify our position that glass business segment has been reeling under acute economic difficulties and market crunch. It is to be noted that as per the interim settlement dated 07th August 2003, both the parties have agreed that after 1ˢᵗ July 2005, they will come together to discuss about the financial stability and profitability of the company and then if required parties will finalise the extension of the same settlement up to 30ᵗʰ June 2006. It is specifically agreed between the parties that workmen covered under this settlement will ensure that they will abide by the terms and conditions of the settlement agreed upon and give guarantee to stability and viability of the company.

The union had agreed for interim settlement dated 07ᵗʰ August 2003 only after being fully convinced about the rationale behind extension of the agreement for one year w.e.f. 30ᵗʰ June 2004.

PENDING PROCEEDINGS BEFORE CONCILIATION OFFICER

Since there is agreement between the management and the Trade Union about the implementation of 9A provisions, the Office of the Conciliation is seized of the matter and subsequently commenced the conciliation proceedings and conciliation meetings have been conducted as per the following details:

DATE	MEETING
19/07/05	*First Conciliation Meeting*
08/08/05	*Second Conciliation Meeting*
18/08/05	*Third Conciliation Meeting*
06/09/05	*Postponed to 20/09/05*

UNION HIGHHANDEDNESS

When the management has shown its readiness to discuss all outstanding disputes with the union, the recent developments in the plant clearly indicate negative and indifferent attitude of the union disregarding the welfare of

1,000 employees, and their dependents as well as stability and futurity of the company.

  i)   *Instigating people to blatantly refuse OT including reliever OT.*
  ii) *Wearing black flag while at work.*
  iii) *Workmen were not available in the work spot at the call of supervisors for doing the assigned job.*

The above acts on the part of the union and its members are the gross violation of spirit of bipartite method of resolving outstanding disputes in a peaceful manner. This is to be noted that instigating people to go on a strike, refusal of overtime shall cause irreparable damage to the continuous process industry like ours. Disruption in the continuous process like ours may cause catastrophic effect in the form of furnace damage leading to loss of production and equipment damage.

MANAGEMENT POSITION

We believe in bipartite discussion with the union to settle this issue amicably for which the management has not closed the doors for mutual discussion. But we made categorically very clearly that the management does not have any bargaining power to commit anything nearer to their demand for an increase of Rs.1,900/– and above due to sheer business reasons. On the contrary, the union has taken a position not to continue the bipartite discussion unilaterally, if the management is not ready to start the negotiation with an increase of Rs.1,900/–.

We will be forced to take drastic measures in the interest of the smooth operation of the plant activities for which the union and its members will be solely held responsible.

- Exhibit Ends -

ANALYSIS OF THE SITUATION

When the ecosystem in the plant is not conducive for direct negotiation or discussion, communication campaign on the part of the management would give employees a fair picture of the prevailing situation. On account of the union prodding/ fear of repulsive stand on the part of the union, even though the employees might not influence a sudden change in the hostile situation, nevertheless, it can create some opinion in the opposite camp to whittle down the extreme course of action. Moreover, appropriate government, a biggest player in any Industrial Relations system, can be kept informed of developments in the plant on account of troubled labour-management relationship.

CAPTION LINEAGE: In the eyes of business continuity, HARD approach of the management would be justified, but from the sociological/ethical/public welfare perspectives, it would lead to perception of antipathy by the principal stakeholders of Industrial Relations System, i.e., government, society, media, etc. So if the HARD approach of management is based on sound judgment and holistic logic, it shall be perceived as RIGHT approach by the principal stakeholders.

Circumventing the Negotiation Deadlock | 4

MANAGEMENT PROPOSAL TO CIRCUMVENT THE NEGOTIATION DEADLOCK CREATED BY VIRTUE OF HIGH COURT ORDER

As the High Court has stayed any action on the part of the management in the 9A notice submitted to the appropriate government, legally no bilateral negotiation can be allowed to take place between the parties until 9A petition is disposed of. Even though the management was not ready to sign the MOM of any bilateral discussion for amicable settlement with the union until 9A petition is withdrawn by the latter, the management has expressed its willingness to resume negotiation to find out common areas of understanding. The intention of the management was two-fold:

1. to reduce the hostilities as far as possible, and
2. to prompt constructive attitude on the part of the union.

Management's Response to Commonly Asked Questions About Wage Settlement

Constant communication is considered to be a prerequisite to convey the right message to the employees particularly when IR issues are at stake. Here the strategy of the management was to focus on certain commonly asked questions by the union and workmen in general. There are two schools of thought about the Strategy of Communication when IR situation is not normal—One argues the fruitility of communication when the opposition camp is not in a position to listen and the other one argues for silent revolution, which happens on seeing the message, which manifests in the form of behaviour either immediately or later. Nevertheless, the management found it rather harmless to communicate certain facts about the ongoing standoff, details of which are furnished below.

Exhibit #3

S.NO	COMMONLY ASKED QUESTIONS	ANSWER BY THE MANAGEMENT			
01	This plant should be treated as separate entity from other units for wage settlement	This plant is a 100% subsidiary of a larger group having the same glass container units in four locations. Workmen at our unit enjoy 25–30% more salary than their counterparts in other three units. This creates administrative and managerial issues. This is because, for thirty-three lines the salary offered is very low than our four lines production.			
Comparative salary statement (CTC-Monthly)					
	Our Plant	Unit 2	Unit 3	Unit 4	Unit 5
Highly skilled	11,256	6,150	8,213	6,250	9,250
Skilled	9,709	5,917	8,011	4,801	8,200

Semi-skilled	8,180	5,806	7,930	4,580	6,300
02	Financial position of our Plant is very good		a) After take over, the company has inherited an accumulated loss to the tune of 140 crores. b) Cost of critical inputs for the plant has gone up substantially. The company has incurred an additional expense of over 10 crores in 2005 for the procurement of critical inputs compared to 2003 (price increase chart appended below).		

Additional financial commitment—Raw material—Price increase (PMT) Period Sept'03 to July'05

RAW MATERIAL	SEP '03 PRICE	JUL-05	DIFFERENCE	%	AVG MLY CONS	ADDITIONAL COST
Calcite	1,849	2,030	181/–	10	330	597,30.00
Dolomite	1,371	1,452	81/–	6	280	22,680.00
Limestone	1,402	1,422	20/–	1.5	669	13,380.00
Feldspar	1,638	1,806	168/–	10	356	59,808.00
Cullet	2,762	3,087	325/–	12	2,410	783,250.00
Sheet glass	2,138	2,567	429/–	20	350	150,150.00
Selenium	875	7,500	6,625/–	758	120	90,960.00
Soda ash	7,352	9,447	2,095/–	29	969	2,030,055.00
Furnace Oil (KL) April'04-July'05	9,270	15,278	6,008/–	65	885	5,317,080.00
Additional monthly cost escalation						8,527,093.00
Annual additional cost burden						10.23 crores

		c) The investment of fifteen crores in labelling plant is proven to be a dead investment owing to the down fall of soft drinks business segment. d) The company has rebuilt the furnace by spending a whopping amount of Rs.85 Crores in anticipation of high Sales performance but due to market slump it is not materialised. e) Cost of production has gone up by 10% and sales realisation has come down by another 6% in the recent time.

COST Vs SALES REALISATION

Month	Cost of production (PMT)	Sales realisation (PMT
April '05	10,923	12,453
May '05	11,348	12,101
June '05	11,782	11,862
July '05	12,038	11,795
	10% increase in	6% decrease in SR in

All these factors add to the financial position of the company very badly.

S.NO	COMMONLY ASKED QUESTIONS	ANSWER BY THE MANAGEMENT
03	Management staff is getting more and workmen are paid less	a) Employees in an organisation will get the salary as per their qualifications, attitude, skill, experience, competencies, etc, as well as risk involved in the job. b) As far as management staff is concerned, they are not protected by any labour law and they are always running the risk of losing the job at any moment. c) Like other workmen, they should be eligible for annual increment and promotion. But, management staff were denied any annual increment and promotion during 2000–2001 and 2002–2003. d) The management does not have any workman qualified to be considered for officer grade, based on qualification, experience, skill, and attitude.
04	Cost of living is high and hence the management should offer more in the settlement.	a) At present, the company is paying Rs.7/– per DA point which is the highest one comparable with our group companies. In all other units, the amount paid per DA point ranges from Rs.1.50 to Rs.2.60. By any yardstick, the DA given by the company is fairly on the higher side. In other words, DA takes care of occasional price increase and annual increment takes care of loyalty of person to the company. So where is the question of high wage rates without considering the ground realities of our business.

05	Last agreement, workmen were offered Rs. 1,900/– even while the company was not making any profit	a)	In fact as per the last agreement, productivity improvement measures were agreed including reduction of manpower from the surplus area. To be very precise, actual average increase was about Rs. 1,000/– only.
		b)	The formula agreed was out of every 3 rupees, 1 rupee should go to wipe off the loss (140 crores), 1 rupee goes to productivity improvement and the balance 1 rupee goes to wage increment.
		c)	No company can afford to sign a wage agreement without considering present market conditions, future growth, productivity, quality, cost, and profitability. What prompted an MNC to sell its holding to national level group?
			The answer is sheer nonperformance. The present management thinks not only for the short-term business but also for the long-term survival.

- Exhibit Ends -

Employee Welfare—The Organisational Stand

The management is really committed to look after the welfare and security of employees and their family members. Let us look at what the management has done for its employees. Even with a staggering accumulated losses of Rs. 140 crores, the management went ahead with Rs.85 crores investment which in turn has ensured absolute security to the employees for the next ten years. If the market hopefully becomes better, the management has no hesitation in pumping further funds. The management is pumping another Rs.13 crores so as to bring down the cost of production and make the unit viable. The commitment of the management is there to be seen in actions.

Let us look at two aspects of any employee–employer relationship viz., Welfare and Discipline.

The management is committed to the welfare of the employees through providing security, imparting value-based knowledge, and ensuring the safety at the workplace. If the financial position of the company becomes comfortable, maybe four to five years later, it will extend further support.

The management is also firmly committed to the discipline of the organisation. The management firmly believes that discipline alone can bring about the long-term future for this organisation. Hence, other than the statutory rules and regulations, this organisation will run on the terms and conditions of the management. If there is any challenge to the discipline of the organisation, it will be dealt with severely. You have the past records to support. We, as management, look at 'losses incurred for imposing just discipline as an investment for a better future.' We will stick to this principle in totality, as the future of the organisation is the future of those employed with it.

All these point to one basic fact that 'the management has got faith in their employees'.

However, it is observed that some section of employees are in favour of agitation programmes against the management.

Any such agitation programmes or protests shall be seen as acts of indiscipline and hence will be viewed very seriously by the management. The union and workmen will be held squarely responsible for any consequences, which may arise of these measures.

Therefore, the union and its representatives must see wage negotiation in a flexible, reasonable, and constructive manner based on 'Give and Take' principle for the long-term growth of the company and its employees.

OUTCOME OF COMMUNICATION AND FLEXIBLE STAND ON NEGOTIATION:

Although the above-mentioned strategies worked, they were not effective enough in terms of changing the ground situation. The situation continued to be tense with no let up in display of offensive posters by the union and workmen. Perhaps it generated a sort of discussion among some section of workmen to explore conciliatory approach to solve the outstanding differences.

SHOP FLOOR IMPACT: QUALITY AND PRODUCTIVITY

The prolonged standoff had started taking its toll in terms of shop floor quality and productivity.

- Shopfloor workmen resolutely started producing defective bottles.
- Slow down of the production operations causing low productivity.

- Obstruction to the movement of materials to outside job work, as part of normal days' operation.
- Refusal of overtime on critical operations.

The situation appeared to be very serious and the management was forced to issue the following circular highlighting the deteriorating situation.

Exhibit #4

INTERNAL CIRCULAR

1. REFUSAL OF OVERTIME/RELIEVER OVERTIME: The workmen have been continuously refusing overtime including reliever overtime. It is reported that 288 production hours have been lost on account of overtime refusal by the workmen till 07/01/06.

2. POOR EFFICIENCY OF PLANT OPERATIONS: The workmen have been indulging in slow down of the plant operation with effect from 29th December 2005. As a result of slowing the production activities down, the forming efficiency has been remarkably reduced from the average 86%–90% to 75%–77%. The company is incurring huge financial loss and plant inefficiency on account of this unwarranted action by the union and its workmen.

3. DETECTION OF THE CRITICAL DEFECTS IN GLASS BOTTLES FOR FOOD PRODUCTS: It is consistently reported that shop-floor workmen have been found indulging in making glass bottles by paying scanty attention to quality parameters prescribed in this regard. As a result of dereliction of duty on the part of workmen, it is apprehended that these glass bottles produced for food product may contain glass particles (spikes) which are considered to be highly injurious to the safety and health of the consumers. So the management restrained itself from delivering the defective bottles for ultimate use by the customer.

4. ATTEMPT TO OBSTRUCT THE MOVEMENT OF COMPANY MATERIAL: *On 6th January 2006, Mould Shop workmen have made an attempt to obstruct the movement of casings from the company to outside job work. If the casings are prevented for job work outside, it can lead to nonavailability of cavities/ moulds for the production of the glass bottles.*

The Honorable High Court has given direction to the employer not to remove raw materials and machineries from the company's premises, in order to avoid labour unrest. A copy of the interim direction of Hon. High Court restraining the union and its members from indulging in unfair labour practices and wrongful trespass is enclosed herewith.

'We would like to reiterate the point that castings are not raw materials, but are very critical accessories for the manufacture of glass bottles. And this, in no way, is acting against the judgment of the High Court. We would like to bring to your kind attention that, any further attempt to block the movement of the material from the factory to outside job work will be handled with firm hand by the management.

Cooperation from the law-and-order agencies is already sought via our letter dated 07.01.2006.'

- Exhibit Ends -

CONTINUED PRODUCTION OF QUARANTINED BOTTLES

Even after having been sensitised on production of defective materials, the situation continued to be grim as there was no let up in the production of defective bottles. This prompted the management to come out with another circular and personal campaign (along with other management teams) so as to apprise the dangers involved in production of glass bottles with spikes. The contents of the circular are furnished below:

Exhibit #5

INTERNAL CIRCULAR

It was reported that on 7th January 2006 "A" shift glass bottles produced for certain food products have been quarantined on account of critical defects. Surprisingly, the bottles with critical defects have been located in the packed ware. There is every reason to presume that the Forming and Cold End Sorters in Lehr number-11 have flouted their duty of quality inspection.

It was also observed that, in the last couple of days, health drink bottles produced by us were also having critical defects on their surface. Such defects pose dire health hazards to the infants, students, and adults who consume these health drinks as there is every chance of glass particles getting mixed.

Please note that critical defects of glass bottles meant that these food products can lead to prohibitively alarming consequences including loss of human life. This sort of duty dereliction can eventually lead to criminal offence if the company fails to supply glass bottles without such grave defects.

Recently, it was reported that a glass company had to pay Rs.15 lakh rupees to its customer who lodged a complaint against the presence of spikes in the glass bottle. Fortunately, the customer could identify spikes before they were ingested and thereby saved the precious life of his family members.

It is to be borne in mind that industrial dispute should not result in the loss of human lives on account of dereliction of duty by the employees. If there is negligence, sabotage, and dereliction of duty on the part of employees, it can lead to serious consequences. Therefore, it is forewarned that any such act of sabotage and dereliction of duty by our workmen should not be tolerated by the management and it will be managed with heavy hand particularly to avoid loss of confidence of customers and criminal prosecution proceedings against the management and its employees.

- Exhibit Ends -

PARTIAL SUSPENSION OF PLANT OPERATIONS

It is important to highlight that, in any furnace-driven glass factory, if the output is less than the prescribed limit, then there is likelihood that the furnace may develop thermal shock leading to fire hazards that would harm, not only the internal precincts but also the neighbouring places.

In spite of repeated communications and discussion with the union, the disturbed IR situation had been affecting the productivity as well as the quality of incoming materials from the lines. In addition to this, workers manhandled the trainees who attended overtime to maintain line productivity.

Beyond business interests, what worried the management was the safety issues in operating the plant below the rated capacity. It may be noted that, instead of 330 MT (rated capacity of the furnace), all the four lines taken together had started producing less than 180-200 MT per day. As per the technical specifications for the safe operation of the plant, the production should not be less than 220-230 MT per day.

Low productivity coupled with safety hazards, poor quality of glass produced, and related IR incidents are inimical to the healthy shop floor management. The management of the unit decided to partially suspend the operation of plant.

> *CAPTION LINEAGE: There was no room for SOFT approach on the part of the management when the union and its affiliates got indulged in rampant unfair practices, which eventually made it impossible for the management to continue with the production operations. HARD hitting approach was contemplated by the management in partially drying one line of operations to give a message to the employees and the union that management never tolerates rampant indiscipline and unfair labour practices.*

The notice published by the management to partially suspend the operation of the plant is appended below:

Exhibit #6

DRAINING OF MACHNE NO.11
NOTICE

The employees are aware that our factory which is engaged in the manufacturing of glass containers is a continuous process due to the fact that the heart of the operations, the furnace, which is used for melting silica sand, etc, into molten glass, has to be kept in operation continuously.

The recent events that have unfolded and the conduct of the workmen are completely demoralising to the management.

The workmen are aware that the Company has ever since its commercial operations have been incurring losses. The workmen are further aware that the company which has spent more than 85 crores in rebuilding the entire furnace and other infrastructure in the hope to make the Company revive the losses incurred by increasing the production/ productivity.

While so, the workmen have recently on the issue of charter of demands, resorted to concerted refusal to do overtime work including reliever overtime, which is necessary particularly in the light of the continuous nature of operations of the factory. Several notices put up by the management did not yield any fruitful result. Though such concerted refusal have been going on ever since the middle of September 2005 and which has resulted in huge losses to the management, in the hope that the workmen and the union would see reason in their action, countenanced patience.

The workmen have ever since 26.09.2005 resorted to slogan shouting, using abusive language at the officers and mass indiscipline of loitering and wasting time during working hours apart from continuing to refuse overtime work, even in cases of exigencies.

On 15.10.2005 and 26.10.2005, the workmen have without any provocation and all of a sudden, resorted to gheraoing the senior officer and the officers were kept confined for several hours. They have collectively squatted on the floor outside the room of the officers, preventing the officers from ingress/egress. Several workmen are also found freely loitering in the factory including areas where the inflammable material are stored, thus, gravely endangering the safety of the materials stored there. The entire climate has become very volatile inasmuch as unruliness has become the order of the day and the workmen, without any restraint, are found to be at places where they are otherwise not required to be. The workmen have also been challenging the authority of the superiors when questioned about this or when asked to do their normal work.

Your kind attention of all concerned are fervently solicited in our letter addressed to various authorities as per the following particulars. Police Department and Labour Department vide our letters dated 17.10.05, 18.10.05, 20.10.05, 25.10.05, 26.10.05.

The workmen, however, in gross disregard to the critical financial position of the company, had made a demand of 40% bonus, despite the fact that the Provisions of the Bonus Act had no application to the workmen employed in our factory. Even when the financial of the company in the last few months shows financial losses, the management has agreed to pay the maximum of 20% (Bonus + Exgratia) on the conditions that the union and its members restore the normalcy and continue to maintain the same till the amicable settlement of long-term agreement. The copy of normalcy agreement has already been sent to Labour and Police authorities vide our letter dated 29th November, 2005.

In contravention and gross violation of normalcy agreement, the union and the workmen have resorted to Over Time refusal including reliever Over Time, threatening the trainees, adopting tactical moves with ulterior motive in disturbing normal production w.e.f. 29.12.2005. The management has displayed the current industrial relations update to enable the workmen to understand the present situation and communicated the same to all authorities concerned vide our letter dated 30.12.2005. Subsequently, they have been continuing slowdown of operation and thereby contributing colossal financial damage and day to day plant operations have been found to be crippled. Normal plant average efficiency in the range of 82 to 87% per day has come down to 55%, 65%, and 73%. Every one percentage (1%) drop in efficiency is adding one crore loss to the revenue position of the company on monthly basis.

Above all the workmen on the shop floor have resorted to dereliction of duty particularly quality inspection and checking. As a result, on 7th January, 2006, in First Shift (A) at line no.11 glass bottles for food products have been found to be quarantined due to critical defects, etc., presence of glass particles inside the glass bottles. If anybody consumes the food products, there will be an imminent danger to human life and can be interpreted as prosecutional offence by the employer and employees. On 8ᵗʰ January at line no.11, the efficiency is only 47% with held ware quantity of 35%. On 9ᵗʰ January, First Shift (A) packing efficiency is only 19% and there has been no let up in the tight situation caused by the go-slow tactics, Overtime refusal and dereliction of duty by the workmen. In spite of hourly notice put up by the shift engineer on 10.10.06 the management has been forced to cullet the defects because of continuous defiant stand taken by the union and workmen.

Under the above circumstances, the management is compelled to drain line no.11 of the factory with immediate effect.

Since each line is whole unit consisting of Forming, Sorting, and Packing, dereliction of duty in any one of the sections by the workmen can contribute to making the whole line ineffective, unproductive and unviable.

The workers being engaged in the same line are producing defective bottles against the management's instructions, tantamount to refusal of assigned work.

The management would review the suspension of operations until it is assured of unconditional cooperations from the union and its members for the viable operation.

- Exhibit Ends -

APPRISING LABOUR COMMISSIONER AND POLICE COMMISSIONER OFFICE

Management has not lost any time to inform Labour Commissioner and City Policy Commissioner about the situation, which prompted the management to suspend the partial operations of the plant.

The report contained the following aspects:

- normalcy agreement signed for bonus disbursement wherein it was explicitly agreed by the union to abstain from unfair labour practices including refusal of over time;
- lower plant productivity and consequent impact on the operational viability of furnace;
- safety hazards in operating furnace below the rated capacity;
- production of inferior quality bottles and its impact.

As appropriate govt. and law and order machineries play a vital role in resolving the standoff between the management and the union in any IR situation, the above intervention by the management would be termed as absolutely proactive and appropriate.

Contents of the letter framed by the management is reproduced below for having an accurate assessment of the ground situation.

Exhibit #7

1. *The union and its workmen indulged in overtime refusal and other unfair labour practices to get bonus during the last Deepavali season. In spite of difficult financial situation, the company has paid <u>20% (bonus and ex-gratia)</u> irrespective of provisions as per the Payment of Bonus Act. This was done despite the <u>normalcy agreement</u> wherein the union and its workmen have agreed not to indulge in any activity prejudicial to production and productivity.*

2. *In violation of normalcy agreement, again the union and its workmen have started go slow, overtime refusal and other unfair labour practices from <u>29th December 2005 onwards. Every day the company has been suffering huge loss on account of these activities.</u>*

3. *In furnace driven continuous glass industry like ours, the furnace is required to be kept in constant high temperature and in order to heat the furnace at the required temperature, flammable materials such as LPG and furnace oil are to be used. If the furnace is allowed to function below the minimum draw in a day, it shall produce <u>thermal shock</u> and also likely to cause the huge <u>fire mishap</u>. In that eventuality, <u>it would be disastrous to the property of the factory as well as surrounding environment.</u>*

4. *They have started producing defective bottles meant for food industries. The bottles contain spike and glass particles. It will affect the safety of the consumers and endanger the lives of people as it*

poses severe health hazards. The employer will be prosecuted for criminal offence. The previous acquisition happened in 2002 particularly on account of failure on the part of the former owner to run the business in a viable and productive way.

5. *The last wage agreement signed by the management with the union has provided pay hike irrespective of productivity, cost consideration, quality parameters etc., Expecting pay hike without any meaningful contribution in improving productivity and profitability of the company is unsound proposition in running glass factory particularly under the following situations:*

   a) *Profound decline of carbonated soft drink business segment.*

   b) *Escalating cost of raw-materials particularly furnace oil and LPG.*

   c) *Imminent threat from substitute product like pet.*

6. *The workmen have started the agitation in support of their charter of demand. The management is interested in signing productivity agreement and thereby share the gains which result out of it with the workers. But they are unable to take any decision on productivity proposals.*

7. *Out of 4 production lines, the workmen have continuously produced the defective bottles for food products in uncontrollable limits in one (1) line. It is presumed that this is an act of sabotage under the connivance of the company union. Thus, the production activities have become unproductive, uneconomical, and unviable.*

8. *The Hon. High Court has issued interim direction restraining the union and its members indulging in unfair labour practices. The Hon. High Court has also directed law enforcement agency to provide adequate protection to the employer against any unfair labour practices and activities prejudicial to the production and productivity being committed by the union and its workmen.*

In view of the continuous generation of defective bottles, it became unviable for the management to run the production line. Consequently, the management has stopped one production line on 10th January 2006. For the above act of in-discipline, the management has resorted to suspending two workmen, which was not accepted by the union.

In view of threat perception and apprehended troubles by the workmen, your good office is requested to direct the concerned government agencies to provide adequate and necessary protection if the union and the workmen indulge in unfair and prejudicial activities as well as in the case of suspension of business operations by the company due to continued slow down and other unfair labour practices.

- Exhibit Ends -

UNION–MANAGEMENT INTERFACE POST DRAINING OF ONE LINE OF PRODUCTION

The management was expecting that the union would approach the whole issue in a very pragmatic manner and thereby pave the way for negotiated peaceful settlement. Nevertheless, the union acted in a very smart way. The basic concern of the union was payment of wages to the workers deployed in the suspended line of operation. Even though the management was trying very hard to impress upon the union the very impact of continued production of quarantined bottles and low productivity, the union representatives rather adopted a nonchalanting and indifferent approach to the main issues governing the very survival of the plant operations. They were found to be involved in unleashing a campaign that the management is interested in closing down the unit rather than amicable solution of the industrial dispute.

It was very categorically informed to the union that the payment of wages of the workmen working in the suspended line of operations was not plausible as they were found involved in refusal of reasonable order of the supervisors to maintain the shift productivity and quality and as such no-work–no-pay norm would be enforced. There was a sort of no-holds-barred argument on this aspect of payment of wages between the management and the union which further led to the division of interest and vitiated an atmosphere of peaceful settlement.

> *CAPTION LINEAGE: No doubt the HARD stand taken by the management is justified because of the unfair labour practices of the union and the workers which left the management with no option other than taking a tough stand.*

Discussion with Chief Minister of the State

The management had sought an appointment with the Chief Minister and explained to him the deteriorating IR situation in the factory. The management representatives carried a sample of defective and quarantined bottles produced by the shift workers just to apprise him the highhandedness on the part of the union. This was followed by meeting with Labour Commissioner, Labour Secretary, Senior Superintendent of Police, and other government officials.

Suspension of the Whole Plant Operations

Ever since the closure of one line of operations, the situation continued to be very challenging to run the plant operations because of the following reasons:

- Go-slow by the workers: Efficiency of line productivity has gone down from average 82%–85% to 55%–71%. As the whole line pull was very much below the minimum required pull of 230 MT, it was running the risk of furnace damage and consequent safety hazards.
- Disruption/slow down of production and movement of moulds from Mould Shop to production has made the situation very difficult even to maintain below-average productivity. Unless the production department gets the mould design from the Mould Shop, it is proving to be very difficult for the production department to produce the bottles with required market specs.

- Transgression of normalcy agreement at the time of bonus settlement wherein the union has agreed to maintain the status quo until the final settlement is arrived. Consequently, there used to be blatant refusal of overtime, continued slogan shouting and gate meeting which eventually proved to be very much disruptive in terms of peaceful atmosphere.

- Continued production of defective and quarantined bottles leading to the disruption of delivery schedules to the customers.

CAPTION LINEAGE: No doubt strong action of the management (in partially draining the operations) had failed to evoke positive response from the union or the union might unable to turn around the opinion of their members towards constructive solution. HARD approach of the management in the given situation to suspend the whole plant operations is to be seen from this angle.

Barely 14 days after stopping the production of one line, the management found it prohibitively difficult to run the normal operations of the plant and declared full suspension of plant operations. Circular issued in connection of suspension of plant operations is reproduced below:

Exhibit #8

Internal Circular

Suspension of plant operation on account of continued go-slow agitation and unfair labour practices by the union and workmen.

The employees are aware that our factory which is engaged in the manufacturing of glass containers is a continuous process due to the fact that the heart of the operations is the furnace which is used for melting silica sand etc., into molten glass has to be kept in operation continuously.

The management believes in peaceful and harmonious coexistence with the union and the workmen. The recent events that have unfolded and the conduct of the workmen are completely demoralising to the management.

1. *Concerted go-slow agitation w.e.f. 29.12.2005*
2. *Refusal of reliever overtime and overtime.*
3. *Obstructing the movements of cavities to outside job works for the production of varied glass bottles to meet the customer demands.*
4. *Working against the basic interest of the Company and General Public by producing defective glass bottles with spikes and glass particles, despite the fact that our end production is predominantly used for consumer industry, thus posing a grave threat to the end user.*
5. *Wilful go-slow in mould machining area, thus deliberately creating scarcity of Cavities / Moulds required for production of glass bottles.*

6. *Disrupting of works and activities prejudicial to production and productivity by blatantly violating the normalcy agreement reached with the management dated 27.10.2005 for Bonus/Exgratia disbursement.*

7. *Late reporting, Grouping and loitering inside the factory premises during working hours.*

The combined impact of slow down and misdemeanour on the part of workmen has created a situation wherein the management could not run ONE production line out of FOUR lines effective 10.01.2006 on account of production of defective bottles for food industries and reduced efficiency.

The management has given the union and the workmen sufficient opportunities to prevail upon them good sense but to no avail.

On 23.01.2006 the management has decided to discontinue the operations in Machine No.12 on account of scarcity of mould being created by the slow down agitation by the Mould Shop Department.

Workmen attempted to ensure normal supply of moulds in the other machines, however, even this was of no avail, as the supply of moulds required for production continues to be in short supply due to the rampant go-slow adopted by the workmen.

Being a continuous process industry, the draw of molten glass from the furnace for production would have to be maintained at a prescribed level, as otherwise, it could pose a serious risk of fire hazard. Technically, if the draw from the furnace is less than the rated minimum of 225MT per day against the prescribed pull of 330 MT per day, it can lead to THERMAL SHOCK as likely to cause risk hazards to the Plant and Machineries and People besides neighbouring locality given the fact that it is having storage of LPG, HSD and Furnace Oil. Significantly low pull can also damage the furnace which has been recently modified at the cost of Rs. 30 crores.

By considering abnormal cost of production due to drop in production and efficiency levels, risk and safety hazards, and non fulfilment of customer needs in quality and quantity in time, the management is compelled to SUSPEND THE OPERATION of the entire PLANT with immediate effect.

Needless to state that the management would review the situation upon an assurance form the workmen and the union to restore normal production.

- Exhibit Ends -

Business HR Interface Before and During Labor Unrest | 5

IR issues have the potential to reverse business prospects in a direct manner. Generally, a professional approach, which integrates Business and Workers' interests, is likely to provide an ecosystem conducive for sustainable growth. This when translates into reality, it is said that behaviour of the unions/workers across bargaining table is the manifestation of managerial policies and practices in governing them. If it is progressive and constructive, then there is every likelihood that there exists industrial peace. Most often, how HR professionals take a strategy by integrating these two vital dimensions determines the effective shop floor behaviour. It implies very authentic Business and Welfare Champions role that HR needs to play for symbiotic Business HR interface.

Here are a few live incidents to emphasize on the imperatives of synergistic Business HR interface.

MANAGING GHERAO

While the standoff between the management and the union over the long term became intense, the bonus issue came up for discussion. Prior to the year 2005, the workers got 16.66% bonus whereas on account of tightened business scenario coupled with labour unrest, management took a position in one of the bipartite discussion that minimum bonus of 8.33% only would be payable during the financial year 2005. Several rounds of discussion did not bring any reconciliation between the parties.

It is customary to distribute bonus in the plant prior to Deepawali by the companies. As the bonus issue was kept pending till 4 days before Deepawali, it was a sort of testing time for the management and the union to check the uprising emotions on the part of workers. One fine evening, when Senior Management officials were meeting Govt. officials outside the company, suddenly a call came from the Plant that workers started gheraoing Unit Head in his chamber with abusive slogans and agitated mood.

HR Head and other officials of the company then decided to return from the City to tackle this crisis situation at the plant. While returning to the plant, several calls came up suggesting that situation is really very alarming and agitated workers may try to manhandle, vandalize etc.

As the Unit Head was gheraoed by the workers, there was an apprehension that HR officials will not be allowed to go inside the room where the agitating workers held the Unit Head under the siege. But contrary to the expectation, HR officials had the leeway to go inside. Meanwhile, local police officials were also inside the plant premises as per the request of the management.

The management had made it very clear to the police officials that unless the workers in the shift duty go back to the place of working, there is no question of any discussion with the union on the bonus stalemate. Since the management did not show any let up in its stand, the union officials asked the workers to resume shift duty and they resumed. Only then, the management representatives agreed for a discussion with the union on the bonus issue.

After a protracted negotiation with the union representatives, the management had agreed to pay 20% bonus to all workmen based on the belief that it would pave the way for peaceful IR situation and end of hostilities in vogue over the delay in Long term settlement.

BUSINESS IR INTERFACE

- No talk of bonus settlement unless the workers go back to the place of work by withdrawing the siege created in the Unit Head's chambers. This along with the insistence on the bonus settlement to the effect that 2.30 hours' salary would be deducted from the worker's salary as they were found absconded from the workplace for gherao.
- The above along with normalcy agreement reached with the union leadership wherein workmen agreed not to indulge in activities inimical to the production and productivity (like OT refusal, go-slow tactics, slogan shouting, black flag protest, etc.).

> *CAPTION LINEAGE: Permanent way to end any IR standoff relies to a great extent on the swift move of the management not to surrender its prerogative to manage an undertaking under pressure from the union's arm-twisting strategies. In the absence of HARD approach, there observed to be no alternative.*

EGRESS OF FINISHED GOODS OUT OF FACTORY PREMISES DURING THE SUSPENSION OF OPERATION

Movement of finished goods out of factory premises during the suspension of operation. How this can be made possible? Here also interfacing role of HR with Business needs to be highlighted particularly in the context of troubled IR situation.

An HR with a strong sense towards business needs, in times of troubled IR situation, should resort to quick and logical ways to resolve it. When there was a sort of requirement on the part of the management to egress the finished goods out of factory premises during the course of its suspended animation, HR had been after various legal agencies to find the way out. After due deliberations with all, it was concluded that legally all glass containers manufactured prior to date of suspension of operation can be sold out on commercial terms to the clients. Further it was clarified that factory is only in suspended animation and not closed. As such, the business operation is in vogue and only manufacturing operation alone is kept under the suspended animation.

Next question is how this can be achieved particularly when the workers are on war path? Some of the major clientele for whom the company supplied the finished goods were found to be in operational crisis for want of glass containers. Among other customers, industry big players were hit the worst by nonsupply of glass containers. The company management has approached these companies and obtained letters from them highlighting production difficulties for want of glass containers, filed an affidavit with the High Court seeking injunction order from the court to restrain agitating workers not to come in the way of egress of finished goods manufactured before the suspension of operations of the plant and kept in the warehouse. The injunction order has clearly directed the government to provide necessary police protection to carry out the operations on a daily basis.

But the government and police department were observed to be very apathetic to the court's directions as the elections to the state's legislative assembly was around the corners. If any untoward incidents happen, the government would be branded as antilabour. As such, the company management had not received any support from the government and local police officials. Again, the company management moved the High Court seeking explicit direction to the government for providing police cover for finished goods movement.

Police had no option other than providing protection for finished goods movement. On an eventful day, about sixty police personnel were deployed to send the outside vehicle inside for finished goods movement. HR Head was reviewing the situation at his residence. His residence was virtually converted into a control room as the factory was in suspended animation. On his residential line, SP of police, on cell line, company's director from Kolkata, and on his personal mobile line, Unit Head of the company were all hooked in. When the agitating workmen were preventing the vehicle to go inside the plant for finished goods movement, SP of police was seeking permission from HR Head to arrest the workmen for the its smooth passage. SP had no other choice than to arrest the workmen failing which the police department/government would be accountable to judiciary for a contempt petition at High Court. Meanwhile, director and Unit Head of the company were continuously pitching in quite often with clear mandate to arrest the workmen. In spite of overwhelming compulsion for arrest, HR Head simply suggested to maintain the status quo in the high drama situation.

Some deliberation is required as to what prompted HR Head to take a call to maintain the status quo in spite of the fact that law-and-order machinery was fully in favour of the management to arrest the workmen.

> Had the arrest happened, it would have generated bad blood in labour management situation as the management needs to work with the same class of people at the time of resumption of plant operation.
> Who will bear the cost of incarceration of more than 75 to 100 agitating workmen for two weeks? Arrest for contempt of court involves lengthy legal process of bail out.
> Probably would have antagonised police machinery and government department.

Post this incident, HR Dept. had launched a publicity offensive against the union for the contempt of court and disrespect shown to the rule of law. While all leading newspapers did cover/publish the news items, HR Dept also sent fax messages to the governor, CM, Industries Minister, Labour Minister, Labour Secretary, Labour Commissioner, DIG of Police, etc.

This publicity offensive was proven right in not only isolating the union for the contempt of the court but gained confidence of the government machinery to marshal the support for the management's position. Next day, when the management was trying to send the vehicle inside the plant premises, there was absolutely no commotion created by the agitating workmen sans even slogan shouting against the management.

BUSINESS IR INTERFACE

- HR proved to be very effective in getting the Interim Injunction order from High Court for finished goods movement when the factory was in suspended animation. Probably for first time in the history of IR standoff in the company, commercial transactions happened resulting into the stock out position of close to 1,800 MTS of glass bottles, resulting in good sales turnover even while the factory was in suspended animation.
- Influenced the position of external stakeholders of the company like government, law and order department, and local public more favourably towards the company apart from giving a psychological blow to the union and its future plans.

> - Gained the confidence of some segment of the workmen aligned with the union who favourably disposed towards the management.
> - Winning the goodwill of the workers on a long-term basis to settle the outstanding differences.

> *CAPTION LINEAGE: The management is expected to take SOFT or HARD approach considering the short- and long-term consequences. In spite of the precipitation, the police failed to take any direct action against the workmen. Can we term this decision of HR as SOFT approach? If the HARD decision of the management disturbs the basic fabric or foundation of Industrial Relations, it must desist from taking such HARD approach. If the SOFT approach is going to culminate in HARD benefits in terms of greater realisation on the part of the union and a strong message to the principal stakeholders of Industrial Relations system, then SOFT approach is always preferable.*

MISSION LPG TANKER

Suspension of operation of any furnace-driven glass plant completes only when draining of molten glass operation is completed followed by cooling operation to avoid imminent furnace damage as a result of thermal shock. For cooling operation to happen in a smooth manner and in a controlled setting, sufficient quantity of LPG and water are to be made available. Around 450 MT of molten glass at 1,450°C to be drained out post suspension of operation.

As the workers and the union representatives were on sit-in agitation at the company entrance, the situation was proving to be extremely difficult for the management to take LPG tanker from outside for cooling the furnace post its draining. Even the management approached some of the Internal Union leaders to prevail upon the workers to let the LPG tanker in the factory premises which went unheeded.

Meanwhile, HR and other top management officials were in close touch with state administration and police department for their help and protection to carry the LPG tanker inside the factory premises as the workers were found to be very belligerent in disallowing the tanker to go in the plant. Surprisingly, police officials were found to be wanting in extending required protection. The situation became so intolerable that the cooling operation has to happen on the war footing basis without loss of any further time failing which 8.5 crores furnace may develop cracks due to the damage of refractory.

HR officials decided to meet police top brass in the state administration and the Lieutenant General. Sustained efforts really gave some results at the end of a series of parleys. Police convoy was allowed with special protection force armed with weapons to facilitate LPG tanker lorry to go inside the plant premises. At the same time, HR officials also got in touch with local police personnel to have an informal campaign with agitating workers in front of the company gate not to create any disturbance for the movement of LPG tankers inside the factory premises. This two-pronged strategy proved right, and simmering tension compounded in the minds of top management officials got settled with the safe passage of the LPG tanker for the controlled cooling of drained furnace.

BUSINESS IR INTERFACE

- Timely decision on the part of HR to meet up with TOP police officials and gubernatorial person has helped the management to avert imminent danger to the lifeline of any glass factory, i.e., the furnace.
- Support from the government machinery coupled with campaign by the local police created a permissive atmosphere for the LPG tanker to go inside without any untoward incident.

Preserving the functional efficiency of the lifeline of a glass factory, i.e., the furnace, is considered to be a critical aspect of managing a glass plant. The management would have never expected any role for support services like HR to play in this area. Yes, Mission LPG has proven to be yet another pointer that only proactive HR can intervene timely and meaningfully to ward off any extreme repercussions having potential to disturb the basic foundation of an organisation.

CAPTION LINEAGE: More than HARD or SOFT approach, the proactive role played by the HR proved to be very effective in preserving valuable equipment from the imminent danger of developing cracks which might lead to dangerous unsafe consequences not only for the plant but also for the neighbouring inhabitants.

POTABLE WATER AND THE AGITATING WORKMEN

With the suspension of plant operation, workers had no option other than to put up a brave front in the eyes of the public and the management. As expected, the union had set up a protest camp (shamiana) just in front of the main entrance of the plant and started mustering the strength of the workers. On an alternating basis, the union office bearers and workers used to sit in the camp and chalk out the next action plan. The union collected money from the passersby apart from their own contributions. The collected money was spent for making light food for those who were in the protest camp. For first two days of suspension operations, the security of the company allowed taking potable water from the company meant for cooking purpose by the workers as there is no other source of water in the nearby area. After two days of suspension of operations, essential goods like rice, milk powder, etc., were found to be in short supply for the crew inside the plant (engaged in draining operations of the furnace) and workers obstructed supply of these essential items meant for them.

The management representatives then informed security people to stop the supply of potable water and accordingly the management abruptly stopped potable water supply for their use. This led to some anxious moments for the union officials as they were finding it difficult to organize drinking water for cooking. The management stand also was not in favour of restoring water supply to them, as their main motto was to weaken the morale of the workers.

The situation became intolerable for the workers and HR representatives started getting frequent phone calls not only from the internal Trade Union members but from External Union leadership as well. HR Manager had taken a decision to restore the water supply. Though initially the HR Manager had to face the wrath of the management, subsequent events buttressed the fact that it proved complementary for the management, particularly for the safe draining of the furnace.

BUSINESS IR INTERFACE

- In spite of pressure from the workers, the union leadership prevailed upon them to allow essential goods for the crew stationed inside the plant.
- Certainly facilitated in providing some thaw in the heightened tension between the management and workers.

In IR, these kinds of genuine considerations on the part of either of the parties would certainly pave the way for permissive climate to weather the storm. The outcome may not be immediate but surely acts as a subconscious trigger in the minds of people to dispose favourably in a given situation.

CAPTION LINEAGE: This SOFT approach in terms of basic human considerations need not be seen always from IR perspective. Behaviour based on genuine human considerations would have either short-term or long-term connect for sure.

Voice of the Management Being Heard in the Union General Body Meeting

Even after a lapse of three months from the suspension of plant operations, there was not much of voice in support of revocation of suspension of plant operations. At times, the management was also bewildered to come into terms with this reality irrespective of the fact that majority of the workers wanted the plant to reopen at the earliest.

On the basis of continuous feelers, it was concluded that probably the voice of majority of workers was not heard in the Union General Body meeting being organised frequently to decide upon the future course of action. The main trigger which paved the way for suspension of operation was the union's stance on 9A provisions and the management's stance on implementation of 9A provisions and readiness to discuss only productivity-based proposals in place of any blanket increase in the wages without any rationale.

Having understood that the union is trying to mislead the workers, the HR Dept officials started working towards making the workers realise through some internal common sources their willingness to discuss productivity proposals. Also the workers started approaching the HR Dept with a request to end the stalemate on the account of their deteriorating financial background.

It is to be mentioned that the union office bearers wantonly did not disclose the willingness of the management to discuss productivity proposals with the workers. Having sensed this, HR Dept officials started spreading the willingness of the management to discuss productivity proposals with the union through some of the Junior Management representatives who were in touch with workers regularly. Meanwhile some of the workers started approaching the HR Dept with a request to end the stalemate on the account of their deteriorating financial background. Through them, too, the HR Dept officials intimated the willingness of the management to discuss productivity proposals.

Meanwhile, External Trade Union officials were evincing keen interest to resolve the stalemate with HR Dept. The HR Dept conveyed its willingness to have open dialogue based on mutual give and take through them as well, however, they made it very clear that productivity should be the basis of wage hike.

By and large, the willingness of the management to discuss productivity proposals was communicated to the majority of the workmen and external Trade Union officials. It is to be highlighted that General Body meeting of the union was dominated by a few office bearers and their cronies. In the euphemistic language, these people are known as Hawks who seldom take strong positions to resolve the deadlock.

Amidst suspension of operations, a tough call was taken by the management to terminate the services of one office bearer of the union by resorting to 'Discharge Simpliciter' provision as per the ID Act 1947. The rationale to invoke Discharge Simpliciter was corroborative evidence collected by the management against him for his involvement in the disruptive acts prior to the suspension of operation as well as his vehement opposition to the peaceful settlement of the ongoing impasse.

As far as Discharge Simpliciter is concerned, it is not enforceable by law. Apex Court in the country has turned down many pleas in favour of Discharge Simpliciter by citing the reasons well known in the context of Principles of Natural Justice. Nevertheless, for reasons best suited to the given situation and considering the larger interest of the organisation and employees, the management decided to remove him from the services by invoking the provisions of Discharge Simpliciter.

This really acted as a bolt from the blue for the union as it really pre-empted the moves of hawks to go ahead with their nefarious designs.

BUSINESS IR INTERFACE

1. Sensing the appropriateness of the situation, HR Dept acted very swiftly to dismiss an office bearer of the union which has really helped to create a facilitative environment for exploring ideal options for mutual coexistence. It requires robust decision-making capability in a trying situation while seeing the ramifications of the same in future.

2. Timely communication measures unleashed by HR to inform basic facts involving the management–union interface helped to create essential understanding of the ground realities among the majority of the workers and thereby making sure the voice of the business is heard in the union forums.

CAPTION LINEAGE: HARD decision taken by the HR to dismiss an office bearer of the union by invoking certain typical clause in the Industrial Disputes Act proved to be a big jolt and it created some kind of introspection among the office bearers about their future strategies to be adopted in overcoming the current impasse.

HAWKS TRYING TO CONTROL
THE GENERAL BODY MEETING

In the intervening period, a couple of General Body meetings were organised to strategise the union's response to the management and thereby explore the possibilities of reopening of the plant.

In spite of the above outlined measures, hard-core elements in the union were observed to be very much determined to thwart any positive response from the union to the management. These elements were very vociferous not to dilute the union's earlier stand and proposals made to the management.

As the time was running out for the management to take a crucial decision to continue with the plant operations, at a high level meeting chaired by the director of the company, it was decided to give statement of reasons of its proposed decision to close the plant operations to the Labour Department. This step precedes actual notice of closure as per the Section 25FFA of Industrial Disputes Act.

The statement of reasons submitted to the Labour Dept. for the management's intention to close down the unit is furnished below:

Exhibit #9

<u>REASONS FOR CLOSURE</u>

This group was taken over in 2002 particularly on account of failure to run the business in a viable and productive way. The last wage agreement signed by the management with the union dated 9th April 2001 for a period from 01.07.2000 to 30.06.2004 has provided pay hike averaging Rs.2,200/– (CTC) per employee. Since the earlier management wanted to transfer the ownership of the company during the same period, they did not bother and were not serious about viability and economic aspects of the glass business. The last agreement was extended for another twelve months by signing 12(3) agreement dated 7th August 2003. This extension of agreement was considered necessary particularly by the Trade Union because of declining business prospects, heavy competition, unfavourable external factors including import of cheap glass containers from China and other European countries.

Having understood the tough scenario in glass business, the management had been very much proactive in advising and telling the union about the need for increased performance and productivity much before the expiry of the settlement, 30th June 2005.

Subsequent events unfolded in the company show that the company union and its workmen have adopted unhealthy, unfair, uncooperative, obstinate, and adamant stand and thereby resulting into suspension of plant operations w.e.f. 25th January 2006. In the light of the above, the management is constrained to serve the closure notice as it has been finding no improvement in the attitude of the union and the workmen towards the management in running the glass plant in an economically viable manner.

The reasons for intended closure of the Glass Containers plant are enumerated below:

1) 9A Notice And Pending Procedures Before Labour Conciliation Officer

The management issued 9A Notice dated 5th July 2005 to the union stating that in order to sustain the viability of the unit due to poor sales realisation, cost incurred (to the tune of Rs.85 crores in the rebuild of furnace in 2003, dumping of glass containers of Chinese origin, the management has no other choice but to cut down cost drastically wherever possible and however small. As per the last bilateral settlement, it was mutually agreed that canteen subsidy and transportation subsidy could be revised at two intervals. But the management did not revise those subsidies keeping in mind larger welfare of employees. 9A Notice issued by the management contains nothing abnormal except to go by what was agreed earlier between the management and the union plus other legally defined and acceptable measures including leave provisions and holidays provisions as per relevant labour laws.

In continuation of 9A Notice issued to improve the operational viability and stability of the company on long-term basis, the union had given a strike notice dated 6th

July 2005 to the management and subsequently the matter was referred before the conciliation officer for pending resolution. The office of the conciliation was seized of the matter and subsequently commenced the conciliation proceedings and the conciliation meetings conducted as per the following details:

Date	Meetings
19/07/05	*1ˢᵗ Conciliation Meeting*
08/08/05	*2ⁿᵈ Conciliation Meeting*
18/08/05	*3ʳᵈ Conciliation Meeting*
20/09/05	*4ᵗʰ Conciliation Meeting*

The above details clearly demonstrate the facts that the Labour Department had given enough opportunities for the union to discuss the matter with the management for the peaceful resolution of 9A dispute. Eventually, the conciliation meeting failed to arrive at any solution and office of the conciliation has served a failure report dated 27ᵗʰ September 2005 to both the parties and appropriate government.

2) Union Highhandedness

During the pendency of conciliation proceedings, the union and its workmen were found to have indulged in the following unhealthy and unfair labour practices vitiating the climate for a mutual resolution of 9A dispute.

    a) *Instigating the people to flatly refusing overtime including reliever overtime.*

    b) *Wearing black badge while at work.*

    c) *Workmen not being available in the work spot at the call of supervisors for doing the assigned job.*

Details of overtime refusal were made known to Labour Department by our letter dated 22/09/05.

3) Permanent Injunction Order

On account of the above activities and apprehended violence and demonstration on the part of workmen, the management had issued a circular dated 14th Sept 2005 reminding the union and workmen about the illegality of their activities as per the Permanent Injunction Order No.46 of 2001 dated 30th April 2001 received from the Hon. Court of Additional Sub-judge. As per the permanent injunction order, the following acts or deeds on the part of anybody shall be construed as contempt of court.

1) *To conduct strike or demonstration at any place within a radius of 200 metres from the factory premises.*
2) *Obstructing or preventing any officers, staff, servants, and other workmen in discharging their normal duties.*
3) *Obstructing the movements of machineries and other materials to and from the factory.*
4) *Affixing posters, handbills, etc., in the notice.*

But unfortunately, the union did not give even a scanty attention and thereby involved in activities prejudicial to the basic spirit of permanent injunction order. Office circular to this effect was issued dated 26th Sept 2005.

4) Industrial Relation Situation Report—I

The IR situation report—I containing the activities of the workmen prejudicial to industrial harmony, orderly progress of the work, efficient performance of the plant, and productivity was prepared and sent to Labour Department dated 14ᵗʰ Sept '05. The IR situation report—I highlighted apart from overtime refusal, included the activities presumed to be violating the spirit of permanent injunction order issued by the Hon. Court of Additional Sub-judge.

5) Overtime Refusal and Imminent Danger to Safe Operation of Plant and Machinery and Safety of Employees

Since the union and workers reported to have indulged in overtime refusal without any provocation, the management apprehended the safety hazards in running the plant and machinery. The company is using highly inflammable substances like LPG, furnace oil, and HSD and at any given point of time stores about 60 tons of LPG, 520 KL of furnace oil, and 280 KL of diesel. These are all highly explosive substances and have the potential to catch fire and eventually can end in a major fire catastrophe, if the areas are manned inadequately in all shifts. It even has a potential to spread fire and thereby cause irreparable damage to the life and property of the people living in nearby village hamlets.

6) Industrial Relation Situation Report—II

The IR situation report—II containing the activities of the workmen prejudicial to the basic safety and security of the plant and machinery, people, and nearby village area was made known to the workmen via office circular dated 22ⁿᵈ Sept '05 and the same was given to the Labour Department.

7) Intervention by the Management to Apprise the Critical Situation to the Workmen

In spite of sincerely trying to convince the union and its members about the difficult situation experienced by the management, the workmen refused to perform overtime including the reliever over time in critical sections like electrical, machine maintenance, and furnace between 13.09.05 and 16.09.05 which might cause unimagined and dangerous consequences and eventually lead to major catastrophe. They were also informed that the management might be compelled to take severe measures including suspension of operations for which the union and its workmen shall be held squarely responsible.

8) Appeal by Company Vice President

An appeal was issued to all workmen dated 22ⁿᵈ Sept '05 by vice president of the company briefing the current situation and lower productivity by the workmen and thereby putting the plant into indefinite losses which will lead to extreme and unavoidable step of shutting down the plant.

9) Industrial Relation Situation Report—III

The IR situation report—III contained the seriousness of the situation caused by the continued indulgence of overtime refusal including mandatory overtime by the workmen. It was also highlighted that refusal of overtime might lead to running the factory in minimum capacity by consuming excessive fuel inputs resulting into unviable operation of the plant. The copy of the IR situation report—III was also sent to Labour Department dated 26th Sept '05.

10) Incident of Physical Assault

On 16th Oct 2005 at 10.05 p.m., the shop floor workmen gathered in the forming department and committed verbal and physical assault to a technician trainee without any provocation. Thereafter, he was menacingly threatened not to report this matter to higher ups. This incident of physical assault of technician trainee was adequate enough to create fear psychosis among other workmen. This incident in the shop floor had vitiated orderly arrangement of daily work schedule and facilitative climate for mutual discussion.

A warning notice has been displayed at main entrance notice board and issued the same to the union and its members for their reprehensible and dastardly offence committed against their fellow workman. The matter was also made known to Circle Inspector of Police dated 17th Oct '05.

11) Provocative Incident on 15th Oct 2005

On 15th Oct 2005, a group of 35–40 were workmen found to have indulged in slogan shouting and provocative speeches and thereafter squatted in front of the HR Department and subsequently aired their protest against the slow progress of bonus discussion. This was in spite of the fact that the management had already negotiated with the union and made its stand very clear for bonus payment.

This incident reflected abject failure of the union to control and discipline the behaviour of its own members to redress their grievances by lawful and constitutional means.

12) Industrial Relation Situation Report—IV

IR Situation Report—IV dated 18ᵗʰ Oct 2005 containing incident of physical assault incident, provocative behaviour, statistics showing impact of overtime refusal and other provocative behaviour of workmen was sent to Labour Department.

13) Incident of Gherao on 26ᵗʰ Oct 2005

The union and its workmen ('A' and 'B' shifts) indulged in unfair labour practice of gherao in front of CGM's office on 26ᵗʰ Oct 2005. This happened irrespective of the fact that bilateral discussion for bonus agreement was in progress with union. The workmen who were egressing after 'A' shift duty and those who were ingressing for 'B' shift duty and 'G' duty workmen found to have gathered in front of CGM's office and forcefully entered into his room and started gheraoing from 2.00 p.m. to 5.00 p.m. Due to nonavailability of workmen in the shift, daily production was severely affected. This unprecedented behaviour on the part of the union was absolutely uncalled for especially when the bilateral discussion happened with the union for bonus settlement.

14) Bonus Settlement

In spite of adverse financial condition and continued indulgence in unfair labour practices by the union and its workmen, the management had agreed to pay 20% bonus and token gift worth Rs.200 each to all the workmen on the condition that the workers will restore the normalcy and cooperate with the management in arriving at long-term agreement peacefully. To be more specific, restoration of normalcy implies the following:

1) *Withdrawal of overtime refusal.*
2) *Withdrawal of slogan shouting and black badge protest.*
3) *Restraining other forms of unproductive behaviour such as threatening, physical assault, etc.*

A copy of the bonus agreement was sent to Labour Department on 29th Nov '05 for necessary information.

15) Industrial Relation Situation Update

Update on current industrial relations situation, by including the following details, was sent to Labour Department dated 30th Sept '05.

a) *Raw-Material Price Escalation*
b) *Sales Realisation*
c) *Fall of Glass Industries*
d) *Threat of Globalisation*
e) *Interest Servicing Burden*
f) *Fall of Soft Drinks Segments*
g) *Salary Structure of Workmen*
h) *Normalcy Agreement*
i) *Permanent Injunction and Management Position*

16) Permanent Injunction
Order Issued by the Hon. High Court

Permanent injunction order was issued by the Hon. High Court, dated 5th Dec '05 in favour of the management and thereby restraining Trade Union or its workmen from indulging in any activity which is considered to be prejudicial in running the business smoothly, including productivity and plant performance.

17) Go-Slow Strike from 29th Dec 2005

The trade and its workmen were found to have indulged in go-slow strike with effect from 29th Dec '05 by blatantly violating normalcy signed with the management and permanent injunction order issued by the Hon. High Court. As result of slowing down the production activities, the production efficiency was remarkably reduced from the average 86%–90% to 75%–77%. This caused huge financial damage to the company.

18) Critical Defects in the Glass Bottles

Apart from go-slow strike, the plant workmen were found to have indulged in making glass bottles meant for food products with critical defects. Glass bottles produced for food product containing glass particles (spikes) are highly injurious to the safety and health of the consumers. This reported behaviour on the part of shop floor workmen to make glass bottles with critical defects for client use generated unprecedented apprehension on the part of the management about the quality parameters to be scrupulously observed while manufacturing glass containers.

19) Obstruction of Movement of Vehicles from the Company

It was reported that on 6ᵗʰ Jan 2006, Mould Shop workmen had made an attempt to obstruct the movement of castings from the company to outside job work. If the castings are prevented for job work outside, it can lead to deficiency of mould for the production of glass bottles. This behaviour on the part of workmen was found to be violative of temporary function order issued by Hon. High Court.

20) Industrial Relation Situation Report—V

IR Situation Report—V was sent to Labour Department dated 7ᵗʰ Jan '06 by incorporating the following details:

1) *go-slow strike,*
2) *critical defects in glass bottles, and*
3) *the incident of obstructing the movement of company materials.*

21) Internal Circular Dated 7ᵗʰ Jan 06 Highlighting the Impact of the Bottles Produced with Critical Defects

An internal circular was issued by the management highlighting the implication of the bottles produced with critical defects. There was enough reason to presume that the quality inspection to be carried out by Forming and Cold End sorter Lehr. No. 11 *have flouted their duty to do quality inspection diligently on 7th Jan 2006 'A' shift. It was also observed that the health drink bottles produced by the workmen were found to be critically defective. The circular also highlighted that the consumers of health drinks are mostly infants, students, and adults and may run severe risk of health hazards by consuming the contents mixed with glass particles. The tool proof pack ware audit by the company management prevented the products from going to the end users, which otherwise would have caused an unprecedented crisis including criminal prosecution against the employees and the management.*

22) Negative Impact of Go-Slow Strike on the Plant Performance

It may be recalled that the performance of soft drinks segment was totally in a poor shape due to unprecedented demand reduction. Added to that, whatever little order we were having, the management was unable to execute it on account of go-slow strike and agitation of the workmen. The performance of the division was adversely affected on account of the following reasons:

1) *continual overtime refusal including reliever over time;*
2) *unauthorised absenteeism without sanction/prior information to the supervisors;*
3) *wilful negligence to comply with quality parameters;*
4) *production of defective bottles;*
5) *noncooperation in carrying out supervision instruction from time to time; and*
6) *late reporting for duty and taking excessive time for lunch interval.*

The combined impact of all these activities created production shortfall, production of bottles with defective quality and reduction in plant efficiency which ultimately resulted into financial loss to the tune of Rs.1.75–Rs.2.00 lakhs per day.

A detailed account of the impact of go-slow agitation in the plant was sent to Labour Department dated 7ᵗʰ Jan 06.

23) Continued Generation of Defective Bottles, Poor Forming Department Efficiency and Packaging Efficiency

In spite of genuine request and fervent appeal made by the management, it was unfortunate that the union and its workmen were not responding positively in controlling production of defective bottles and improvement of plant efficiency. This was particularly very much visible in Machine No.11 where the held ware percentage went up from 3.4% to one time high of 78.2%. A detailed account of the Machine No. 11 performance from 22ⁿᵈ Dec '05 to 08ᵗʰ Jan'06 was displayed on the notice board. Copy of the same was also sent to Labour Department dated 10ᵗʰ Jan '06.

24) Issue of Warning Message

The management issued a warning message through a separate circular on 7ᵗʰ Jan '06 highlighting the concerns of the management and the negative impact and repercussions, which might arise due to continuous generation of defective bottles produced by the workmen in Machine No. 11. Even the circular forewarned the employees that if defective bottles are produced for the food industries, the management will be prosecuted by civil and law and order departments of the government in case of loss of life by consuming the products packed in defective bottles.

25) Communication to the Union

The management handed over the written communication dated 10th Jan '06 to the union highlighting the problems faced by the management to run the plant smoothly, including continued generation of defective bottles. The management also requested the cooperation from the union to restore the normalcy on an emergency basis so as to avert the imminent crisis situation.

26) Obstruction of Movement of Semi-Finished Moulds

A group of mould shop workmen gathered in front of mould shop and prevented the movement of semi-finished goods (cavities) for outside job work. This was against the spirit of permanent injunction order issued by the Hon. High Court. Moreover, the group of mould shop workmen behaved in an indecent manner by using abusive language and threat of physical assault and even barged against the management staff working in the mould shop department. This affected the movement of castings and production of glass bottles. A circular dated 10th Jan '06 was displayed at the notice board and the same was informed to police department.

27) Suspension of Machine No. 11

As a result of continued go-slow strike, average plant efficiency in the range of 82%–87% per day had come down to 55%–76%. It may be noted that every 1% drop in efficiency would result into heavy financial loss effecting the revenue position of the company.

Above all, the workmen on the shop floor were found to have resorted to dereliction of duty particularly in the area of quality checking and inspection. As a result on 7ᵗʰ Jan '06 in 'A' shift, line no.11 glass bottles for food products were found to be quarantined due to critical defects, i.e., presence of glass particles inside the glass bottles. In glass industries, the production of critical defects is ruled out under any circumstances. If anybody consumes the food products, then there will be imminent danger to human life and can be interpreted as prosecutable offence being committed by the employer and employees. On 8ᵗʰ Jan '06, again, the efficiency was only 47% with held ware quantity of 37%. On 9ᵗʰ Jan '06, there was packing dereliction of duty by the workmen. This happened in spite of the hourly production bulletins released by the shift engineer in the plant. The management was left with no other option but to drain Machine No.11 of factory on 11ᵗʰ Jan '06. Notice to this effect was displayed in the main entrance notice board.

The photographs of rejected and quarantined glass bottles were reported to Commissioner of Labour.

28) Forceful Entry of Suspended Workmen

Two workmen who were suspended on 10ᵗʰ Jan'06 for their dereliction of duty and misconduct entered the company premises with support of the company union and created unwanted fear and security concerns among other employees and the management. This act on the part of the union further deteriorated already worsened IR situation in the company. For the next consecutive three days, the suspended employees were found loitering in the company premises. The management did not take any action except registering the police complaint only by taking into account peaceful resolution of all outstanding disputes. Finally, with great difficulty, the management persuaded the union to keep the suspended workmen outside.

29) Go-Slow Strike and Drastic Decline in the Output Produced by Mould Shop

A separate department called mould shop in the company is producing the required quantity and quality of cavities. These cavities are used for production of different glass containers. If there is any delay on the part of workmen at mould shop; it will have a crippling impact on the shop floor leading to abrupt production stoppages. On account of go-slow agitation, the management failed to receive moulds for the production of various glass bottles as per the requirements of customers.

30) Industrial Relation Situation Report—VI

IR Situation Report —VI dated 18ᵗʰ Jan '06 by incorporating the following details was sent to Labour Department:

1) *Declining efficiency in Mould Shop and its impact on daily production schedules.*
2) *Declining efficiency in the plant*

31) Circular on Imminent Danger to Run Plant Operations

Due to nonavailability of required quantity and quality of cavities, there was a shortage of moulds for production purposes. A situation was reached in which no moulds were found to be available for Machine No. 12 operations. All this information was made known to the workmen and the union through a circular dated 20th Jan '06. The circular also highlighted risk hazards of operating the plant with minimum draw from the furnace.

32) Detailed Note on Furnace

In order to produce glass bottles, soda lime silica glass needs to be generated through furnace system. Accordingly, the company took technical know-how from a multinational expert and got the entire furnace designed from the same vendor. Ours is 105 sq.m rectangular enfired furnace with 330 ton/day capacity consisting of melt up tank, working-end forehearth, regenerator entirely made out of costlier refractories imported from Germany. All these refractories are constructed according to the design supplied by the same vendor without much of mortar and/or cement, i.e., with perfection of refractory to refractory with zero joint. These refractories will withstand high temperature around 1,800°C and resistance for glass erosion and corrosion.

Raw materials like silica sand, soda ash, feldspar, dolomite, limestone, cullet, and other chemicals are fed into the furnace on batch basis and melted at 1,650°C to achieve molten glass. This molten glass is sent to working-end forehearth and to forming machine for bottle manufacturing.

To achieve 1,500°C inside the furnace, we have to increase the temperature step by step from 0°C and takes minimum of 21 days. Once the furnace reaches 1,650°C, it should be maintained at that temperature for making glass containers. The life of furnace is just seven to eight years, if the temperature is maintained without shutting down the furnace. Maintenance job of furnace, if any, has to be carried out keeping the furnace temperature 1,650°C only. After eight years, based on the corrosion of the refractory of the furnace, relining may be done at a cost of Rs.25 crores after proper draining of the glass and cooling of the furnace. Cooling of furnace will take minimum of fifteen days. Cooling, heat up, including new material feeding, will be done based on predetermined procedure by experts only.

To make the molten glass, LPG, furnace oil, and diesel are the fuels to be used. To keep the furnace under the safe working condition, the following inspections are to be carried out by the workmen in all the three shifts in all the 365 days of a year.

   a) *Flow of fuel oil*
   b) *Supply of combustion*
   c) *Pressure of the furnace*
   d) *Bubbler movements*
   e) *Glass level*
   f) *Reversal system operations*
   g) *Temperature monitoring and controlling*
   h) *Batch movement*
   i) *Maintenance oil, diesel, and LPG burners*
   j) *Conditions of refractories*

For proper running of the furnace, there are adequate controls, but they have to be constantly monitored.

The above inspection work needs to be carried out regularly with great care and attention. Any lapse due to the labour unrest or strike or concerted action on the part of workmen will lead to collapse of furnace having 330 ton of molten glass of the temperature of 1,650°C endangering not only the men and material of the factory but also surrounding industries and nearby villages since the furnace is surrounded by LPG, diesel, furnace oil pipe lines, and storage tanks.

33) Risk Hazards in Operating Plant with Minimum Pull

The rated capacity of the furnace is 330 MT pull per day. On account of suspension of Machine No.11 operations and continued adverse impact of go slow strike by the workmen, the pull came down to 210–225 MT/day. If the furnace is operated less than the minimum rated capacity, it can lead to thermal shock and thereby endanger the safety and security of vital machineries, installations, people, and neighbouring locality.

34) Misconduct and Unlawful Behaviour of Mould Shop Workmen

On 21.01-06, a group of mould shop workmen stopped the movement of moulds/neck rings to other plant for outside job work. This unwanted intrusion and misconduct into the smooth operation of mould shop affected not only the work schedule of this but also other plants in link with it. The above information was conveyed to the nearest police station through letter dated 22nd Jan '06.

35) *Written Communication to Hon. Minister of Labour*

The Hon. Labour Minister was duly apprised of the current IR situation in the company including technical difficulties (to run the plant) and safety problems being proposed by the go-slow agitation on the part of workmen and other unfair labour practices vide letter dated 23rd Jan '06 and through personal interaction.

36) *Draining of Machine No. 12*

The mould shop activities came down heavily owing to continuous slow down by workmen. As a result of perpetual go-slow strike, critical mould shop activities like shaping, milling, turning, welding, fitting, and grinding and quality inspection were performed below the minimum level of efficiency. Even feeding to CNC machine itself was affected to a considerable extent. The combined impact of all these activities had resulted into nonavailability of required quantity and quality of cavities/mould for production purposes. It resulted into nondelivery of mould equipment to forming department. Under the given circumstances, the management was compelled to drain Machine No.12 w.e.f. 23rd Jan '06. In this connection, we forwarded a detailed note on draining of Machine No. 12 and the same was communicated to Labour Department vide letter dated 24.01.06 and marked a copy to the union.

37) *Suspension of Plant Operations w.e.f. 25th Jan 2006*

As mentioned earlier, manufacturing of glass containers is a continuous process due to the fact that the heart of the operations is the furnace, which is used for melting silica sand, etc., into molten glass and has to be kept in operation continuously. On account of go-slow agitation and unfair labour practices by the union and the workmen, a piquant situation emerged wherein the management was not able to run the plant operations smoothly and in a viable manner.

a. *Concerted go-slow agitation w.e.f. 29.12.05.*

b. *Refusal of overtime including reliever overtime.*

c. *Obstructing the movements of cavities to outside job works for the production of varied glass bottles to meet the customer demands.*

d. *Working against the basic interest of the company and general public by producing defective glass bottles with spikes and glass particles, despite the fact that end production is predominantly used for consumer industry thus posing a grave threat to the end user.*

e. *Wilful go-slow in mould machining area, thus deliberately creating scarcity of cavities/moulds required for production of glass bottles.*

f. *Disrupting of works and activities prejudicial to production and productivity by blatantly violating the normalcy agreement reached with the management dated 27.10.05 for bonus/ex gratia disbursement.*

g. *Late reporting, grouping, and loitering inside the factory premises during working hours.*

h. *On account of reduced efficiency and production of defective bottles, the management could not run one production line out of four lines effective 10.01.06.*

i. *On 23-01-06, the management decided to discontinue the operations in Machine No. 12 on account of scarcity of moulds being created by the slowdown agitations.*

Technically, if the draw from the furnace is less than the rated minimum of 225 MT per day against the prescribed pull of 330 MT per day, it can lead to thermal shock and is likely to cause risk hazards to the plant machineries and people besides neighbouring locality given the fact that it is having storage of LPG, HSD, and furnace oil. Significantly low pull can also damage the furnace, which has been recently modified at the cost of Rs.30 crores. With the suspension of two lines out of four and continued and no letting up of slow down strike by the workmen, the pull from the furnace was reduced below the average minimum level.

Considering all the above factors, the management was compelled to SUSPEND THE OPERATION OF THE ENTIRE PLANT EFFECTIVE 25.01.06.

Office circular to this effect was put up on the notice board and a copy of the same was sent to Labour Office vide letter dated 25/01/06.

38) Misdemeanour Violative of Temporary Injunction Order After the Suspension of Plant Operations

With the suspension of entire plant operations, it was necessary to drain the furnace and adequate time should be given for cooling the same. Otherwise, it not only carries the safety hazards but also runs the risk of damaging the whole furnace system costing 30 crores. As quoted earlier, approximately five to seven days time will be taken to drain the furnace and another twenty to twenty-five days time will be taken for cooling the furnace.

The agitating workmen in front of the main gate did not allow any movement of materials. As a result, the safety team inside the plant was deprived of adequate storage of LPG for the smooth draining of furnace. The workmen turned down even the police officials' appeals. Finally, with the intervention by the higher-level police officials, they allowed the LPG tanker to go inside. Till that time, the safety crew inside the plant was in panic as they were running from the imminent danger of explosion of furnace and the resulting dangerous/catastrophic consequences.

In order to meet the emergency requirements of food and pharma industries, the management arranged the movement of finished goods out of the company premises on the strength of temporary injunction order issued by the Hon. High Court; however, many food industries had to minimise/ abandon their production schedules including that of health drinks because of the situation.

39) Violation of Settlement Reached with DLC on 14-02-06

As the settlement arrived at between the management and the union vide conciliation meeting dated on 14-02-06, the union should cooperate with management staff for doing necessary emergency works including preparation of salary. But all these settlement norms were flouted in a flagrant manner by the union subsequently.

- Exhibit Ends -

IMPACT OF THE NOTICE: MANAGEMENT'S INTENTION TO CLOSE THE UNDERTAKING

The apt description of sequence of events that led to the suspension of plant operation in the notice submitted by the management had triggered volley of urgent measures from the Labour Dept. It was learnt that office of the Labour Commissioner has convened a couple of meetings with the union representatives to overcome the impasse. Subsequently, bipartite meeting was also convened by the Labour Dept. In the meeting, the management representatives made it very clear that Productivity Settlement is the way out and it has an open mind to discuss the productivity proposals to sort out settlement issues.

The notice had sent the chill down the spine of the union circles including the workmen. They were really shocked to learn this latest move on the part of the management.

BUSINESS IR INTERFACE

- The three-pronged strategy appeared to have resulted into change of dynamics in the prevailing IR situation. Communication of the management's intent to discuss productivity proposals, Discharge Simpliciter and notice of the management's intent to close down the undertaking together created a favourable situation to resume the dialogue between the management and the union.

- Having identified the role of handful hardcore elements in the union, which created obstacles for any overtures with the management, the swift action by the management to isolate them proved to be effective in terms of resuming bilateral discussion.

CAPTION LINEAGE: HARD stand taken by the management to send the closure notice to the state government coupled with termination of the union bearers in fact turned the coin against the basic interest of the union and its existence. On the contrary, SOFT approach taken by the management in letting the union know that management is ready to discuss productivity proposals as part of its overall strategy to enter negotiation with the union also proved to be conducive to break the impasse.

GENESIS OF BIPARTITE DISCUSSION

The external Trade Union leadership was inclined towards resumption of bilateral discussion with Unit HR. So much so was the desire of the management that even the external Trade Union leadership apprehended unclear move on the part of some of executive members of the union. Nevertheless, the management decided to establish communication channels with external union leadership. This was based on the premise that any overtures on the part of External Leadership would be backed by Internal Union leadership.

But as a matter of fact, hawks in the Executive Committee of the union still had an edge in the affairs of the Union.

It is to be mentioned that the four months of plant closure had an adverse impact on the economic lives of workers and family members. Amidst this frustration, all the union leadership members feigned to be bold and determined to fight it out with the management.

Talk of Splinter Union

As a counter move to checkmate Union Highhandedness, a group of workers from the current union approached the management with a request to facilitate the formation of another union. Even a few members of the Senior Management team also found it rather expedient to do it. But HR had made it abundantly clear to the management that this sort of shortcut would prove to be very much detrimental to have permanent industrial peace in the plant and will affect the existing chemistry between the management and the union. As a result, the talk of such move has had its natural death and did not come up for discussion anymore.

Later on, workers and union members came to know about this fact and really appreciated the principle stand that was taken by HR Dept.

Subsequently, internal Trade Union people approached HR through informal channels to resume bilateral talks.

BUSINESS IR INTERFACE

- Lasting industrial peace is an imperative for the business organisation to grow and sustain. In managing IR, if the management adopts any impulsive or shortcut approach, this may ultimately prove to be a steamroller over business.
- The role of HR assumes significance in adopting a professional stand keeping in mind interests of both the organisation and the workers.
- IR is a very dynamic concept. If anything is done to change the status quo in union–management front, it has to be on the sound premise to avert unpredictable adverse ramifications.

CAPTION LINEAGE: More than HARD or SOFT approach, principle-centred HR leadership would determine quality of Employee Relations in the company.

OUTCOME OF INITIAL DISCUSSION

Apart from the customary exchange of warmth and goodwill, both the parties agreed to have a framework of priority aspects to be mutually agreed upon which will eventually pave the way for reopening of the plant.

For the Management

    a. Performance-linked settlement

    b. Sharing of canteen and transportation subsidy (9A provisions)

    c. General wage hike

    d. Settlement period.

For the Union

    a. Revocation of the suspension of the union office bearer

    b. General wage hike

    c. Performance-linked settlement

    d. Sharing of canteen and transportation subsidy (9A provisions)

For the management, settlement of performance-linked hike would provide the much needed buffer to decide upon general wage hike. The contentious aspect of implementation of 9A provisions particularly with respect to sharing of future increase in canteen and transportation overheads was also considered as a priority as it heralds a new IR culture by valuing each others' concern on equal footing. Both the above might provide a strong premise to negotiate upon general wage hike and finally to decide upon settlement period which in any case is going to be for more than three years from the existing three-year settlement period.

BUSINESS IR INTERFACE

- At the time of issuing note on management expectations from the unions to sign 12(3) settlement, quality time must be spent with the management by HR to understand business expectations. The very fact that HR did spend considerable time with the management and issued a very comprehensive note on management expectations has contributed to reiterate the above aspects with unions and put them in a very prompting situation to initiate the negotiations with the management. The basic learning is that irrespective if the situation warrants or not, it is absolutely necessary to issue counter-demand notice from the management's side as soon as it receives memorandum of demands from the union. Constructive negotiation across the table happens only when parties in the negotiation make their expectations explicit and no surprises later when the climate becomes conducive for mutual give and take.

- Apart from the above, HR took time off from the management again to understand the approach in the given situation—reopening the dialogue with the union after a long lull and hostilities. This meeting proved very effective in terms of getting authority to commit across the bargaining table. Getting authority to commit across the bargaining tables assumes critical importance in the eyes of the union representatives. Unless management representatives enjoy reasonable degree of delegation, the union perceives that the management representatives enjoy sufficient power to commit in front of the bargaining table, and the deal cannot be worked out as per the emerging situation across the table which in any case was beyond anyone's decipher.

Progress in Negotiation: Performance-Linked Pay (PLP)

Having mutually decided to arrive at a solution for Performance-Linked Pay, HR had spent considerable time with management to offer a framework to be considered by the union. In a very proactive manner, both the management and HR discussed this framework well ahead of the negotiation stage with the union.

Chronology of events which resulted into the acceptance of PLP by the union

❖ Before the suspension of plant operation, whenever and wherever HR had an opportunity to interact with the union office bearers and other workmen, it kept on emphasising the need for PLP as a long-term solution to break the stalemate. Although overtly the union did not accept the proposal, covertly it had created some kind of introspection among them.

❖ The company management had decided to base the negotiation on PLP by benchmarking the proposal with an MNC major in the glass container manufacturing space.

❖ PLP framework would be based on critical operation in the glass manufacturing process, and norms for fixing incentive for other process operations should be based on the derivative of critical manufacturing process, i.e., forming or drying operation.

❖ Any form of PLP would be based on both productivity and quality. The achievement of productivity without quality could not achieve the intended results envisaged in the PLP. As such, the management and HR had worked out an acceptable quality level at various processes in manufacturing operations, pending discussion with the union for final acceptance.

❖ A very special provision was considered for inclusion in the PLP, i.e., absenteeism and leave to be accounted while calculating PLP amount payable to the workmen.

❖ Finally, the data back up for the last twenty-four months involving drying efficiency, batch efficiency, mould shop performance, maintenance (breakdown details of critical utilities and equipment), and cold-end operations had been collected, studied, and analysed to peg the performance index at a level which would be achievable but at the same time stretchable within the maximum capacity utilisation of the plant.

Behaviour of the Union Across the Bargaining Table

As expected, behaviour of both external and Internal Union leaders across the bargaining table over PLP at the initial period was not very favourable vis-à-vis the provisions like proportionate deduction of incentive amount for rejected materials on account of quality-related issues, absenteeism, and ESI leave period. This led to the discussion on payment of incentive on daywise efficiency and performance put up by the workmen on overtime. Intense haggling happened to fix the per cent efficiency to be reckoned for incentive fixation at drying operation and corresponding per cent efficiency on other processes in the manufacturing operations. On an average, each workman would get an average PLP of Rs 8.50/- PM over and above fixed hike in their salary by virtue of 12(3) agreement.

The salient PLP scheme agreed with the union is reproduced below

PERFORMANCE-LINKED PAY
(PLP)—FORMING DEPT

OBJECTIVES

1. To promote productivity and thereby enhance performance efficiency
2. To reward the workmen based on performance efficiency
3. To streamline the entire production activities as per quality systems standards
4. To improve competitive position of the company for long-term business success and profitability

SCOPE

The system tries to envisage two types of PLP:

1. Monthly Performance-Linked Pay
2. Daily Performance-Linked Pay to boost up the efficiency

SALIENT FEATURES OF PLP

1. The calculation of PLP is based on monthly efficiency and daily performance efficiency.
2. Monthly production efficiency and daily performance efficiency will be clubbed together to determine PLP on a monthly basis.

3. Overtime is also taken into consideration. For example, if the X workman has the efficiency of 86% in 'A' shift (scheduled duty) and 90% in 'B' shift (overtime work), the average for the day will be 86% + 90% = 176/2 = 88% and the same will be taken as his efficiency for monthly PLP.

THE CALCULATION OF PLP

Production-linked pay under this scheme will be done on a day-to-day basis and a person will earn PLP amount for the day on achieving efficiency of 81% and above as per the following table:

Productivity Linked Pay Norms

PRODUCTION EFFICIENCY—%	MONTHLY INCENTIVE AMOUNT	DAILY PLP, RS.	TOTAL MONTLY AND DAILY EARNINGS, RS.	NET MONTHLY EARNINGS, RS.
81%	200	0	0	200
82%	220	0	0	220
83%	260	0	0	260
84%	290	0	0	290
85%	330	0	0	330
86%	345	1.5	39	384
87%	442	2.5	65	507
88%	494	2.5	65	559
89%	546	3	78	624
90%	626	3	78	704
91%	690	4	104	794
92%	785	4	104	889
93%	846	5.5	143	989
94%	951	5.5	143	1,094
95%	1048	6	156	1,204
96%	1137	7	182	1,319

97%	1231	8	208	1,439
98%	1304	10	260	1,564
99%	1414	11	286	1,700
100%	1528	12	312	1,840

Leave due to sickness or accident under ESI scheme or any other medical leave or leave for any other reason will be treated as absent under this new scheme:

Productivity Linked Pay Conditions

CONDITIONS PARTICULARS	PLP ENTITLEMENT
➢ Absent for one day without prior sanction of privilege or casual leave from HOD during the month.	➢ Entitled for 75% of net monthly earnings.
➢ Absent for two days without prior sanction of privilege leave and casual leave from HOD during the month.	➢ Entitled for 60% net monthly earnings
➢ Absent for three days without prior sanction of privilege leave and casual leave from HOD during the month.	➢ Entitled for 40% net monthly earnings
➢ Absent for four days without prior sanction of privilege leave and casual leave from HOD during the month.	➢ Entitled for 25% net monthly earnings
➢ Absent for five days and above without prior sanction of privilege leave and casual leave from HOD during the month.	➢ Not entitled for any PLP earnings.

As a special case, PLP is extended to forming department trainees. In the case of resorting of bottles of any machines, the daily efficiency will be calculated after deducting the goods rejected during the resorting within twenty-four hours.

Payment of PLP will be made along with monthly wages on the first of every month.

In case the operator or assistant operator of the IS machine is absent for any reason, the person present on the machine, if he or she agrees to operate alone with the assistance of the operator or assistant operator of the other machine, the PLP (daily and monthly) of absent workmen for the particular day will be divided equally among the three workmen for which the arrangement for clubbing of machines would also be arrived at.

BUSINESS–IR INTERFACE

- Productivity-linked pay is highly necessary in maintaining peaceful IR situation as the terms of payment are based on objective norms and depends on workmen's performance.
- The transformation of work culture at shop floor based on competitive spirit could go a long way in promoting the business interest of any organisation. Productivity-linked pay is a very powerful tool which can positively reinforce the philosophy of 'Doing is Understanding' to the shop floor community.

- Achieving the level of perfection in productivity-linked pay is a continuous journey. As the negotiation progressed, the management realised that productivity-linked pay hinges on basic drying operation of the plant. Unless the drying efficiency is improved, there would not be any commensurate improvement in the subsequent stages in the production processes. Further extending PLP for overtime performance, PLP for daily performance to maintain the upscale performance on a day-to-day basis, etc., are the clauses which the management derived as an outcome of continuous negotiation with the union. In fact, the union is a very rich potential source of information to arrive at a competitive PLP.

- As the name suggests, absenteeism is the antithesis of the term *productivity.* In any productivity-related settlement, there should be commensurate deduction of pay for absenteeism at the shop floor. The union and working class might not realise its importance at the time of negotiation. Here the onus lies with the management to continuously educate them about the ill effects of absenteeism. Incentive payment could not be extended to the workmen who fail to turn up on the shop floor. HR point on how a reliever is deprived of PLP in favour of the absented workmen, triggered some introspection among the union leaders, and finally both the management and the union have agreed PLP for overtime performance as well.

12(3) Settlement Stage | **6**

With all outstanding matters discussed at length with both External and Internal Union officials, the stage had been set for signing 12(3) agreement with labour officials. Just for the sake of academic interest, it is very much desirable to have the following checklist particularly to avoid last-minute surprises and to make sure that settlement is signed as per the agreed terms/conditions on stipulated date and time.

CHECKLIST *(ONLY ILLUSTRATIVE NOT EXHAUSTIVE)*

- Discussed with top management and shared the purported agreement copy with them?
- Received their feedback and got a signoff in writing?
- Discussed with both external and internal union officials?
- Got the signoff from both external and internal union officials in writing?
- Have taken time off to meet labour officials?
- Really listened to them and aligned the agreement clauses as required by various applicable legislations?
- Facilitated/organised informal meeting with labour officials and the union officials to take care of last-minute expectations on both sides?

- More importantly, kept the Labor Minister/Chief Minister of the State duly apprised about the developments.

Last Minute Development: Success Still Eludes

Typically, in a glass factory, furnace is the key manufacturing device to process key raw materials into molten glass. Drain-off and drain-on normally take ten to twelve weeks' time. Considering all events which led to the suspension of operation, the management would also be apprehensive about the resolution of long pending dispute. Although the management had taken certain proactive measures to restart the plant operations, the procurement of refractories to rebuild the furnace had delayed on account of technical reasons beyond the control of the management. As a result, a sufficient quantity of refractories was needed to be imported from overseas.

HR/IR Implications

- Commencement of plant operations would be delayed irrespective of the fact that the factory might be reopened.
- Workers who were to engage in furnace operations and process operations would not get full time, i.e., full work in the absence of full-scale furnace operations.
- No option other than resorting to partial lay off.

BIG QUESTION: HOW WILL TRADE UNION AND WORKERS VIEW THIS CONSIDERING THE HOSTILITIES WHICH BOTH THE PARTIES UNDERWENT?

HR had to communicate this emerging development to the union officials. But as a strategy, it was decided to touch base with external union officials and Labour Dept. officials by explaining the unfolding technical issues associated with furnace operations. Contrary to the expectations of the management, the union leaders (both external and internal) prima facie had acquiesced the concerns expressed by the management to commence the furnace operations.

<u>Union Predicament</u>

- How to sell this idea to the workers?
- Even if they succeed in getting across this message to the workers, how could they keep core workers outside the factory premises especially in the light of the fact that close to six months they had to eke out their living without salary?
- How the union leaders' viewpoints would be accepted by the workers without any pinch of salt?

<u>How it was ironed out?</u>

Although as per the law, the management does not need to pay lay off compensation up to forty-five days if the purported lay off is on account of the reasons beyond the control of the management, HR had succeeded in convincing the top management of the company to pay 50% of their salary to all those workers who had to be disengaged from furnace operations

HR and Union Leadership: Business Partners

- HR did sufficient ground work and identified how many workers in furnace areas would get affected by the delay in procuring special refractories from overseas.
- HR discussed with functional heads and identified opportunities where workers with skill set in furnace areas could be deployed elsewhere. This communication from HR with functional heads helped to reduce the number of workmen to be partially laid off.

The above two initiatives from HR supported the union leadership to sell the message across the union circles in order to get their buy in /acceptance.

The formula reached out with functional heads for engagement of permanent workmen is described below in the form of an exhibit.

Exhibit #10

Details of Furnace Damage

Fort-end side, below burner blocks	Fully corroded (7.5-metre length)
Sidewall (on dog house side)	Fully corroded (2-metre length)
Furnace neck	Multiple cracks almost 15% of that entire peripheral of furnace
All four corner blocks (entire periphery of furnace)	Fully corroded (2-metre length)

Damage to the furnace is caused due to cooling.	If it is normal wear and tear, even patch up work would not be sufficient.

- Exhibit Ends -

MANPOWER DEPLOYMENT AND DISENGAGEMENT: Twelve workmen having seven days of work provided some order is available. After seven days, they shall have to be disengaged unless there is a specific work from other departments suitable for their skill and ability.

FURNACE AND BATCH HOUSE: Ten workmen having seven days of work. Further engagement of workmen in furnace section will begin only two weeks before the expected arrival of refractories.

COLD-END QC AND COLD-END MAINTENANCE: Thirty-five workmen having ten days of work and 16 workmen shall have to be disengaged after ten days and again they will be required for work only when the plant is restarted (when IS machine is ready to produce glass containers). The remaining nineteen people shall have to be disengaged after forty days of plant reopening if arrival of refractories is getting delayed beyond 15th October 2006.

FORMING, MMD, MRS, AND MAINTENANCE DEPARTMENTS: Twenty-seven workmen shall have thirty days' work and shall have to be disengaged if arrival of refractories is getting delayed beyond 15th October 2006.

MOULD SHOP AND FOUNDRY: All the forty-four workmen shall have work for ninety days, and if arrival of refractories is getting delayed beyond 15th October 2006, they shall have to be disengaged for a minimum period of thirty days or more corresponding to the period of delay in getting refractories. This may happen after November 2006 or after January 2007 depending upon the completion of existing work.

The summary of agreement signed with the union through conciliation machinery is reproduced below as an exhibit.

Exhibit #11

NONEMPLOYMENT

24.1 The union and workmen are aware that in view of then prevailing situation during January 2006, the furnace had to be drained forcefully and as a result of which damages to the furnace required to be assessed. Further, as the refractories are required to be replaced depending on the assessment of the damage and as these refractories will have to be sourced from various parties and upon the same being available, the minimum period of twelve weeks would be required to recommence the furnace operation even on a minimum scale. As such, work will not be available for the entire workforce upon recommencement of operation and workmen have to be reengaged in a phased manner. Although the management strives to make available required refractories from more than one sources at the earliest, the probability of further delay cannot be ruled out. In such eventuality, the workmen who are allowed to work at the beginning of the plant reopening might have to be disengaged from the work.

24.2 Under these circumstances, the workmen and the union agree that upon the workmen being called for work in a phased manner, as may be deemed appropriate, the workmen will report accordingly. As regards the other workmen who are not called for work due to the reason aforesaid, or subsequently disengaged, these workmen would be deemed to be in nonemployment situation, which is considered to be beyond the control of the management and therefore 'No Work No Pay' principle is applied. But however, based on the request made by the union and workmen and on humanitarian ground, they would be paid a sum equivalent to . . . % of the normal wages (Basic + VDA Only) till the date of these persons being called for work or reengaged, as the case may be.

1.3   It is agreed that there shall be no dispute/grievance regarding the number of workmen to be engaged or disengaged by the management as per the requirements from time to time till normal production is recommenced upon receiving the refractories in required quantity. The workmen and the union, having understood the problems faced by the management, agreed to extend their cooperation in this regard.

1.4   It is agreed by both the management and the union that the Commissioner of Labour shall be duly informed about the details of 18(1) settlement being signed in this regard.

It is also agreed by both the parties that once the normal production and plant operations are restored fully, intimation regarding revocation of 18(1) settlement will be given to the Commissioner of Labour.

- Exhibit Ends -

Business-IR Interface Points During Layoff

The stage wherein HR and the union leadership start trusting each other heralds an era where Industrial Relations transforms its character to that of Employee Relations. In our case, paying 50% compensation to the laid-off workers and substantial reduction of workers from getting laid off can be considered the clinching points for Trade Union leadership to earn the much needed acceptance from their rank and file. HR must help the union leadership to win support for their stands from rank and file without compromising business interest and intent.

Business should support HR and HR should support the union leadership which in turn leads to rank and file to support the principled stand taken by the union leadership—a perfect blend of employee relations management towards permanent industrial peace in organisations.

> *Caption Lineage: Very genuine and considerate SOFT approach in terms of compensation plus substantial reduction of workers from laying off really helped to ease out the situation irrespective of last-minute acceptance of the bipartite deal.*

12(3) settlement: Based on Productivity Improvement and Comparable Compensation Benefits to the Workmen

This settlement is considered as historical towards long-term Employee Relations management:

- A very disciplined and professional approach displayed by HR paved the way for a 'Pluralistic Culture' in which conflict of interest is assumed as inevitable but containable through various institutional arrangements such as negotiation and communication strategies.

- Negotiation and communication strategies would lead to desirable impact in terms of mutual settlement only when business sees union presence through HR as a constructive force in Organisational set up. This fundamental shift or tectonic shift happens only when HR champions business cause through top-degree professional commitment based on the time-tested tenets like value-based leadership and concern for business perpetuity.

- When union leadership starts perceiving HR commitment for a business cause, naturally, Employee Relations ground would emerge for a long-term healthy Industrial Relations climate.

- Productivity-based settlement is now considered as de-risking strategy towards business continuity as parties to the negotiation stage start accepting both macro-and microbusiness indices.

- HR as a coach not only confined to 'within walls of business' but 'outside the walls' of business PARTICULARLY various stakeholders in government to create awareness about competitive scenarios and how legal clauses could be interpreted and reinterpreted as per one's own convenience and short-term perspectives in mind.

- For the first time, union leadership and workers learnt that labour welfare is not at all its PREROGATIVE but it is a goodwill gesture on the part of the management to improve fringe benefits for the welfare of employees. IT WAS MUTUALLY AGREED THAT both canteen subsidy and transportation subsidy hike impact will be jointly shared by the management and workers.

The 12(3) Settlement | 7

MEMORANDUM OF SETTLEMENT

No: Date:

Memorandum of Settlement Under Section 12(3) of The Industrial Disputes Act 1947 and Rule 58 of The Central Industrial Disputes Rule 1957 Reached Before The State Commissioner of Labour

Present   Commissioner of Labour

Parties to the Settlement: The Management of xxxxxxxxxx

                                 AND

                                 The Permanent Workmen of
                                 xxxxxx employed at the address
                                 mentioned above represented by
                                 xxxxx Union
                                 (Reg. No. XXXXXXX)

Representing the
Management:
xxxxxxxxxxxxxxxxxxxx

Representing the
Workmen:
xxxxxxxxxxxxxxxxxxxx

CONTENTS

SHORT RECITAL OF THE CASE

1. THIS MEMORANDUM OF SETTLEMENT arrived at xxxxxx on this day of September 2006 BETWEEN M/s. xxxxx registered under the Companies Act 1956 (hereinafter called 'THE MANAGEMENT' having its registered office at xxxxxx and workmen of the company represented by xxxxxx (hereinafter called 'THE UNION')

2. WHEREAS the union issued a Notice of Termination of previous settlement dated 7th **August 2003 vide letter dated 27.04.2005** along with charter of demands for the revision of existing wages and improvement of service conditions, etc., of the permanent workmen for consideration by the management.

3. In order to meet national and international level business challenges as well as to run the plant operation in a viable and productive manner, the management issued notice dated 5th **July 2005** by incorporating certain changes in working conditions of the labour proposed to be implemented by the management. The union gave the strike notice dated

6th July 2005 to the management by opposing the proposed move to implement changes in the working conditions of the labour.

4. The conciliation machinery seized of the matter and conducted several rounds of conciliation between mid July 2005 and end of Sep 2005. Conciliation meeting failed to evolve a consensus between the parties and eventually the failure report was served by the conciliation officer vide letter dated **27th Sep 2005**.

5. The union in the meanwhile filed Writ Petition before the Hon'ble High Court in 2005 and obtained interim stay of implementation of the proposed changes indicated in the notice dated.

6. The workmen and the union, in the meanwhile, in an attempt to press for their various demands, indulged in various practices and also wilfully reducing the output. Although the management made various attempts to make the workmen see reason, such action continued and as a result of rampant indiscipline of the workmen, the management through notice dated 25.01.2006 suspended the operations of the plant.

7. Subsequently, the management and the workmen held discussions before the Deputy Commissioner of Labour and thereafter before the Commissioner of Labour. The parties also held bilateral talks and tripartite talks before the Commissioner of Labour on various dates between .... And as

a result of active participation and intervention of the Commissioner of Labour, a settlement was arrived at ....

8. The union obtained interim stay from restraining the management in implementing the proposed changes in the working condition.

9. The union and the workmen found to have indulged in unfair labour practices like gherao, protest demonstration, refusal of over time, black badge protest, and gathering in groups in working hours, etc. by violating the spirit of the permanent injunction order No. XX of 2001 dated 30th April 2001 received from Hon. Court of Additional Sub-judge by the management.

10. In spite of several attempts by the management, there was no let-up in the situation and workmen continued to refuse overtime even in critical sections endangering plant safety. One incident of physical assault committed by the senior workmen against shop floor trainee was also reported in the month of during the third week of Oct '05.

11. In spite of adverse financial condition and continued indulgence in unfair labour practices by the union and its workmen, the management had agreed to pay 20% bonus and a token gift worth Rs.200/– each to all the workmen on the condition that the workers will restore the normalcy and cooperate with the management in arriving at long-term agreement

peacefully. To be more specific, restoration of normalcy implies the following:

a.   Withdrawal of overtime refusal
b.   Withdrawal of slogan shouting and black badge protest
c.   Restraining other forms of unproductive behaviour such as threatening, physical assault, etc

12. Since the workmen continued to defy the spirit of permanent injunction order issued by Hon. Court of Additional Sub-judge and express agreement for bonus payment, the management approached the Hon'ble High Court praying for injunction order. The Interim Direction order WPMP xxxxxxxx in WP xxxx dated 27/10/05 and the Hon'ble High Court and thereby restraining trade union and its workmen from indulging in any activity, which is considered to be prejudicial in running the business smoothly including productivity and plant performance, issued 05/12/05.

13. The trade union and its workmen found to have indulged in go-slow strike, production of defective bottles, obstruction of movement of vehicles, etc., and thereby caused production bottlenecks including difficulty to run the plant operations in a smooth and economical manner. This highlighted the indifferent attitude of the union even in complying with the spirit of Hon'ble High Court Order.

14. Rampant go-slow strike and other reported unfair labour practices created a difficult situation for the

management to run the plant operation in a safe and secure manner. It is to be noted that if draw is less than the stipulated minimum, the temperature of molten glass being stored in the furnace might shoot up and thereby produce thermal shock and furnace damage.

15. Consequent to above, the management was left with no other option but to suspend the operation w.e.f. 06.00 hours of 25.01.2006 to save valuable human life, machinery, property of the company, and the adjoining locality.

16. Thereafter, the representatives of the management and the union had direct negotiation on various dates on all aspects of terms and conditions of employment including productivity with the intervention of Labour Commissioner and other Labour Dept officials. The parties arrived at the settlement as per section 12(3) of Industrial Disputes Act 1947 on the following terms in full and final settlement of the union demands and the charter of expectations on the part of the management.

I—APPLICABILITY

01. The provisions of this settlement shall be applicable to all existing confirmed and permanent workmen as on the date of signing this settlement as well as those recruited on probation and confirmed thereafter, employed by the Company only at its establishment/factory at ....

02. This settlement, unless specifically provided otherwise, shall not apply to apprentices (both government and company), trainees, probationers, temporary workmen, casual workmen, contractors workmen, and workmen who have been dismissed and have lost lien on their job or have voluntarily discontinued their service or have rejoined prior to the date of execution of this settlement.

03. In the event that by legislation or otherwise, identical or similar benefits have accrued to the workmen under this settlement or enjoyed by the workmen at present as per existing practices are introduced by the state government or the government of India or other competent authority. Workmen shall be entitled to get either the totality of such statutory benefits or the totality of the benefits that are available under this settlement, whichever is more beneficial to the workmen, but not both.

II—BASIS OF THE SETTLEMENT

01. It is agreed that this settlement fully and finally settles all the issues arising out of the Charter of Demands submitted by the union on 27.04.2005 and their subsequent charter of demands submitted on 10.02.2006. It is agreed that all demands raised in the above Charter of Demands and all subsequent correspondence and discussion there on which have not be specifically dealt with carrying in the settlement will be deemed to have raised, discussed

but not pressed, and therefore dropped by the parties in terms of this settlement.

02. It is agreed that this memorandum of settlement between the parties is by way of a package deal and is on the clear understanding that for the period up to the date of this settlement, the management has discharged all its obligations, statutory, contractual, or otherwise, and no claim shall survive in respect of the period up to date of this settlement as this settlement settles in full and final all the demands.

03. It is clearly understood by the workmen that the terms of this settlement are linked to each other and accordingly, no one term is severable from the other.

04. All other pending demands and issues are dropped by the workmen and the union and it is further agreed that there shall be no demand or dispute, which would involve additional financial commitment to the management either directly or indirectly raised by workmen, either by themselves or through this or any other union, during the pendency and subsistence of this settlement.

05. The workmen shall not, in the event of any difference or dispute arising between them and the company or even between the workmen, resort to any means other than those established by law to seek redressal and shall abjure all unfair labour practices.

06. It is specifically agreed that the total monetary benefits given under this settlement will not form

a basis or not to be quoted by the parties in future negotiations on wage revision, etc., that may take place following the expiry of this settlement.

07. In the case of any error of omission or commission as being found in the 12(3) settlement signed between the management and the union, the actual truth or fact (supported by relevant proof /documents) shall prevail upon both the parties and shall be bound by the same.

08. It is explicitly agreed that the union undertakes to maintain and enforce strict discipline among the workmen in the plant for a healthy work culture. The union also requested the management that the charge sheeted workmen before and during the plant suspension of operation might be given one time opportunity to reform themselves by taking lesser punishment for their misconduct. The management has considered the union request in good faith on the condition that the company is free to take any stringent disciplinary action against those charge sheeted workmen if they indulge in any misconduct or commit any form of indiscipline in the future.

LABOUR FLEXIBILITY AND MOBILITY:

09. The union and the workmen agree that keeping in view the market trends in regard to product demands and technological change, the flexibility in work assignment will be continued. The union and the management and the workmen will together work as a joint team and with oneness of purpose

to eliminate all wasteful practice, removal of all restrict practices in order to sustain and improve the production and business performance of the company.

10. The union and the workmen agree that complete job mobility is an integral part of the terms and conditions of the service of the workmen and the management will have the right in respect of mobility of workmen to follow the practice of flexible work allocation and there shall be no refusal to accept changes from allotted work as and when exigencies of work demand.

11. The union and the workmen agree that the company shall be entitled to eliminate, change, or consolidate jobs, sections, departments, or divisions based on the requirements and also to re-deploy temporarily or permanently workmen from one section to another or from one job to another job.

12. The union and workmen agree that in the light of new machinery/plant to be installed, the workmen shall immediately operate/work on new machinery/plant with the total number, manning pattern as solely decided by the management in a fair manner and there shall be no delay whatsoever/loss production/refusal with regard to the same.

13. The management agreed with the union that it shall not resort to any vindictive action against any workmen once the factory is reopened upon the signing of this settlement.

III—OBJECTIVES OF THE SETTLEMENT

01. In the context of growing competition, fast changing technological environment, and the need to retain the leadership position of the company, in the chosen fields of industries, both the union and the management commit themselves to work together with understanding and cooperation to achieve higher levels of production, productivity, and profitability and attain the optimum utilisation of manpower through training, retraining, multi-skilling, redeployment, increased availability of the workmen at the work spot, avoidance of overtime, and redefining of work assignment consistent with the changing product mix and technological processes.

02. The union and the workmen shall extend necessary support and cooperation to achieve agreed norms of productivity in continuous and consistent manner by following the principles of process ownership and continuous improvement.

03. It is agreed by the union and workmen all quality standards and specifications including Human Resources parameters should be diligently followed in achieving departmental productivity levels as mutually endorsed.

04. Both the parties agree to make efforts to identify and eliminate wasteful practices and to improve quality through replacement of outdated methods, equipment, tooling, and systems with more

effective and efficient alternatives. The union and the workmen wholeheartedly agree to cooperate to implement these systems.

05. The union and the workmen agree to bring down the downtime of the plant and machinery to zero level at the earliest by scrupulous avoidance of wastage of materials and reduction in absenteeism.

06. It is emphasised that improved manufacturing system will be able to react immediately to the demands of the market for higher volumes or change in models whenever required. In the present situation prevailing in the country in the wake of liberalisation wherein one has to face stiff competition with multinational giants as well as business uncertainties, best qualities, improved productivity and cost reduction are the important sustaining factors to retain customers and the very business itself.

IV—CODE OF DISCIPLINE

01. The union agrees and assures that all the workmen will be following the norms and rules stipulated by the company, to maintain discipline in the factory, and to ensure harmonious industrial relations. The workmen will cooperate with the management in its efforts to attain the rated capacity, by maintaining discipline, avoiding waste, avoiding absenteeism, and improving production and productivity in such manner as to augment the competitive strength of

the company in the industry. The union also assures that no trade union activity will be carried out which will affect the production, productivity and discipline in the company.

02. The union agrees that enforcement of discipline is the management's prerogative and the union will extend their cooperation in such enforcement and will not sympathise or support anyone indulging in indiscipline or in activities disrupting normal operations.

03. The union and the workmen agree to improve the discipline and maintain the industrial peace and harmony by proper performance of their duties and not resorting to any act of discipline or any act in contravention of the terms and spirit of this settlement. In the unforeseen situation of strike, agitation of go-slow, or gherao, the management reserves its right to deduct the wages of the concerned workmen as may be deemed necessary.

04. The union agrees that the workmen should report for duty at their appointed time in the work spot. The union also agrees that those workmen who are reporting late at the work spot will be liable for disciplinary action including salary cut.

05. The union undertakes to ensure that once the workmen are reported for duty, they should not indulge in loitering of time in the plant premises except the time allowed for the canteen purpose. The management reserves the right to take disciplinary

action against the workmen in case of loitering during the shift hours.

06. The union and workmen agree that the workmen will report for duty during paid holidays as per the production exigencies and requirement of the management.

07. Both the parties agree that the workmen are liable to be transferred from one department to another and one machine to another or from one operation to another in the plant or one unit or location to another within the same group companies.

08. The workmen and the union agree to fully cooperate with the management in all its efforts to introduce, sustain, and operate successfully all systems, work procedures, instructions of ISO as per the quality management system. The union and the workmen agree to undergo necessary training and follow work practices required towards achievement of the quality system standards.

09. It is agreed that the wrong/wasteful work practices and indiscipline activities will be totally eliminated.

10. Workmen shall not refuse any work and/or various related works that are assigned to them by their superiors during their shift hours.

11. The workmen shall not gather in groups or in any combination within the premises of the plant during/after the working hours.

12. No workmen individually or collectively will interfere in the disciplinary proceedings initiated for the misconducts.

13. Workmen shall wear uniform, shoes and other safety devices issued to them before entering into their department and continue to wear while at work.

14. Workmen shall use the safety equipment issued to them while working, failing which they will be liable for disciplinary action and they will be further penalised for any accident, injury due to their negligent working and not using safety equipments/ devices or not following the safe method of working.

15. Workmen in departments/sections shall mutually help in each other's work as a coordinated team when called upon by the superiors to do so, maintain all production operations at normal desired levels to eliminate production losses.

16. Workmen at no point of time will resort to refusal/delayed execution of work that may lead to production/maintenance holdups. Workmen will continue to carry out the jobs in the interest of the organisation and will not link any of their grievances.

17. The workmen should keep their place of work and equipment clean and tidy and in proper conditions and maintain always-good housekeeping.

18. During emergencies or exigencies, the workmen who are assigned to carry out different nature of jobs should accept such assignment without any reservation and without prejudice to their skills.

19. Being a continuous process industry, at the end of each shift, wherever applicable, workmen should hand over the charge of the machines and work in process in running condition to the next shift workmen along with tools, etc. The workmen will not leave the work spot till the reliever takes the charge of the process. If anybody leaves his place before giving charge to the reliever, he will be liable for disciplinary action.

20. The factory being a continuous process plant, no workmen shall refuse to work on overtime as and when asked to stay due to exigencies of work or for any other reasons.

21. It is agreed that in the event of availability of excess manpower on any day in any shift, in any department, the extra manpower shall be utilised wherever necessary depending upon the requirements for smooth running of the departments including the substitution of the shift relievers. In such cases, the workmen will not insist upon continuing in the subsequent shift.

22. The workmen should wholeheartedly cooperate with the security department to prevent theft, pilferages, accidents/dangers/insecurity to the men and machines and property of the company and

be vigilant in this regard and shall report to the management any unlawful activity that comes to their knowledge.

23. If a workman is absent for more than ten consecutive days without intimation or prior sanction of leave, he/she shall be liable to lose his/her lien on the appointment.

24. Spitting inside the factory premises is absolutely prohibited. If anybody is found doing the same, appropriate disciplinary action will be taken against the erring employees as per the following guidelines:

First occurrence in a month	: Strict warning in writing.
Second occurrence—do—	: A fine of Rs.10/–
Third occurrence—do—	: A fine of Rs.100/–
Fourth occurrence—do—	: Dismissal from the service.

Name of the erring employees will be displayed on the notice board.

V—BASIC PAY

01. It is agreed that all permanent workmen whose names are borne on the confirmed rolls of the company shall be given an increase in the basic pay of Rs. 270/– per month with effect from 01.09.2006

02. Consequent to the revision in the basic pay, change in the basic pay details of all confirmed workmen are furnished as per *Annexure "A"* of the settlement.

VI—VARIABLE DEARNESS ALLOWANCE

01. It is agreed by both the parties that existing system of VDA and the calculation of the Consumer Price Index for arriving at VDA (increase or decrease) shall continue for the company workmen without any change based on the Consumer Price Index no. for industrial workers in the city (Base 1982=100) until replaced by a fresh settlement.

02. Computation of average VDA points shall be done on a quarterly basis and VDA payment will be made in the subsequent month of next quarter. Average points of previous quarters will be considered and rounded off to the nearest one rupee. For the purpose of this clause, the payment fifty paisa or more will be rounded off to rupee one and less than fifty paisa will be ignored.

    a) Variable Dearness Allowance at 476 points
       (base: 1982=100)   : Rs.895/–

    b) Rate per point over and above 476 points   : Rs. 7.0

    c) <u>Illustration</u>:

    – Average points for the quarter October, November, and December 2005 = 577 points.
    – VDA for the month of January 2006 = Rs.1,609/– (points increase or decrease: 577 − 476 = 101 points × 7.07 = 714 + 895 = Rs.1,609/–)

VII—MONTHLY ALLOWANCES

1. HOUSE RENT ALLOWANCE:

1.01 It is agreed that all confirmed workmen will be paid House Rent Allowance (HRA) as follows:

GRADE	Present Rate P.M	Amount Increased	Revised Amount P.M
Unskilled	1,010.00	150	1,160
Semi-skilled-I	1,035.00	150	1,185
Semi-skilled-II	1,060.00	150	1,210
Skilled-I	1,245.00	150	1,395
Skilled-II	1,360.00	150	1,510
Skilled-III	1,510.00	150	1,660
Highly Skilled-I	1,570.00	150	1,720
Highly Skilled-II	1,595.00	150	1,745

1.02 This allowance shall not be reckoned for the purpose of Overtime, Provident Fund, Bonus, and Gratuity.

2. CONVEYANCE ALLOWANCE:

2.01 It is agreed that all confirmed workmen will be paid conveyance allowance as follows:

GRADE	Present Rate P.M	Amount Increased	Revised Amount P.M
Unskilled	633.00	50	683
Semi-skilled I and II	658.00	50	708
Skilled I, II, and III	693.00	50	743
Highly skilled I and II	723.00	50	773

2.02 This allowance shall not be taken into account for the purpose of Overtime, Provident Fund, Bonus, and Gratuity.

3. LEAVE TRAVEL ALLOWANCE (LTA):

3.01 It is agreed that all confirmed workmen will be paid LTA as follows:

GRADE	Present Rate P.M	Amount Increased	Revised Amount P.M
Unskilled	264.00	50	314
Semi-skilled I and II	289.00	50	339
Skilled I	364.00	50	414
Skilled II	407.00	50	457
Skilled III	469.00	50	519
Highly skilled I and II	489.00	50	539

3.02 This allowance shall not be taken into account for the purpose of Overtime, Provident Fund, Bonus, and Gratuity.

4. EDUCATION ALLOWANCE:

4.01 It is agreed that all confirmed workmen will be paid Education Allowance as follows:

GRADE	Present Rate P.M	Amount Increased	Revised Amount P.M
Unskilled	264.00	50	314
Semi-skilled I and II	264.00	50	314
Skilled I	359.00	50	409

Skilled II	401.00	50	451
Skilled III	464.00	50	514
Highly skilled I and II	489.00	50	539

4.02 This allowance shall not be taken into account for the purpose of Overtime, Provident Fund, Bonus, and Gratuity.

5. WASHING ALLOWANCE:

5.01 It is agreed that with effect from 01.09.2006 the existing quantum of washing allowance of Rs. 214/– p.m. stands revised to Rs. 244/– (rupees two hundred and forty-four only) per month to all permanent workmen.).

5.02 This allowance shall not be taken into account for the purpose of Overtime, ESI, Provident Fund, Bonus, and Gratuity.

5.03 Workmen shall make their own arrangements to get their uniform washed on a regular basis.

6. ATTENDANCE BONUS:

6.01 It is agreed between the parties that to motivate workmen for regular attendance performance, one day's gross salary as attendance bonus shall be given to those workmen who present for not less than twenty-four days in a given month.

For computing attendance bonus, the components being taken into consideration are Number of days actually present (not less than twenty-four days in a month) + N & F Holidays + Compensatory Off + On Duty.

7. MEDICAL ALLOWANCE:

1.01. It is agreed by both the parties that the workmen who are outside the purview of ESI Act 1948 shall be eligible for a fixed amount of Rs. 309/–p.m. as medical allowance.

1.02. If any increase in the salary ceiling by virtue of amendment in the ESI Act 1948, then the workmen who are already covered under the medical allowance scheme shall cease to become eligible for the medical allowance and those workmen shall be covered under the ESI scheme.

1.03. It is agreed by both the parties that the workmen who are outside the purview of ESI Act 1948 shall also be eligible for Workmen Compensation under Workmen Compensation Policy being adopted by the company.

VIII—DAILY ALLOWANCES

1. NIGHT SHIFT ALLOWANCE:

1.01 It is agreed between the parties that a fixed amount of Rs.6.00 (rupees six only) shall be paid to those workmen who are present in the night shift ('C' shift) work including overtime duty in 'C' shift.

1.02 This allowance shall not be taken into account for the purpose of Provident Fund, Bonus, and Gratuity.

2. MACHINE ALLOWANCE:

1.01   It is agreed between the parties that fixed amount of Rs18/– per shift will be paid to those workmen working in Forming and Machine Maintenance Departments. This allowance is applicable only when Forming and MMD activities are fully operational.

1.02   It is agreed by both the parties that those workmen who are eligible for machine allowance and continuing after their scheduled shift will be eligible for machine allowance for that additional shift also.

1.03   This allowance shall not be taken into account for the purpose of Provident Fund, Bonus, and Gratuity.

IX. PERFORMANCE LINKED PAY (PLP)

The union and the management mutually agreed to implement production-based reward system by adhering to both quality and HR norms towards making the production system in the company more effective and reward oriented.

For the purpose of performance-linked pay, monetary rewards will be determined based on production efficiency level at forming department. Monetary rewards will be determined individually for Mould Shop (CNC) and ACL departments.

I. OBJECTIVES

1. To promote productivity and thereby enhance performance efficiency
2. To reward the workmen based on performance efficiency
3. To streamline the entire production activities as per quality systems standards
4. To improve competitive position of the company for long-term business success and profitability

II. SCOPE

1. The system envisages two types of PLP wherever applicable:

   a) Monthly Performance-Linked Pay
   b) Daily Performance Linked Pay to boost up the efficiency

3. Monthly production efficiency and daily performance efficiency will be clubbed together to determine PLP on monthly basis.

4. Overtime is also taken into consideration. For example, if the X workman has the efficiency of 86% in 'A' shift (scheduled duty) and 90% in 'B' shift (overtime work), the average for the day will be 86% + 90% = 176/2 = 88% and the same will be taken as his efficiency for monthly PLP.

III. GENERAL HR NORMS APPLICABLE TO ALL DEPARTMENTS FOR DETERMINING MONETARY REWARD ON A MONTHLY BASIS

1. Payment of PLP will be made along with monthly wages on 1st of every month.
2. Leave due to sickness or accident under ESI scheme or any other medical leave or leave for any other reason will be treated as absent under this new scheme.

Specific Conditions

CONDITIONS	PLP ENTITLEMENT
✓ Absent for one day without prior sanction of privilege or casual leave from HOD during the month.	✓ Entitled 75% of net monthly earnings.
✓ Absent for two days without prior sanction of privilege leave and casual leave from HOD during the month.	✓ Entitled for 60% net monthly earnings
✓ Absent for three days without prior sanction of privilege leave and casual leave from HOD during the month.	✓ Entitled for 40% net monthly earnings
✓ Absent for four days without prior sanction of privilege leave and casual leave from HOD during the month.	✓ Entitled for 25% net monthly earnings
✓ Absent for five days and above without prior sanction of privilege leave and casual leave from HOD during the month.	✓ Not entitled for any PLP earnings.

IV. THE CALCULATION OF PLP—FORMING/MMD/ MRS DEPTS

Production-linked pay under this scheme will be done on day-to-day basis and a person will earn PLP amount for the day on achieving efficiency of 81% and above as per the following table:

PRODUCTION EFFICIENCY—%	MONTHLY INCENTIVE AMOUNT	DAILY PLP RS.P.	TOTAL MONTLY AND DAILY EARNINGS— RS	NET MONTHLY EARNINGS—RS
81%	200	0	0	200
82%	220	0	0	220
83%	260	0	0	260
84%	290	0	0	290
85%	330	0	0	330
86%	345	1.5	39	384
87%	442	2.5	65	507
88%	494	2.5	65	559
89%	546	3	78	624
90%	626	3	78	704
91%	690	4	104	794
92%	785	4	104	889
93%	846	5.5	143	989
94%	951	5.5	143	1,094
95%	1,048	6	156	1,204
96%	1,137	7	182	1,319
97%	1,231	8	208	1,439
98%	1,304	10	260	1,564
99%	1,414	11	286	1,700
100%	1,528	12	312	1,840

V. OTHER CONDITIONS

01. In the case of power failure, alternate mode of power generation through generation systems available. The time taken to resume the power supply say 5 MTS or 10 MTS will be taken into consideration for calculating shift efficiency.

02. Other departmental parameters like speed, job selection, job change, machine selection, number of section to run, weight, type of bottle, etc., to be decided by the concerned HOD as appropriate.

03. Suspension of machine operations for more than four hours due to any reasons beyond the control of the management and workmen then machine hour lost will be taken into consideration in determining production efficiency.

04. Effective hot-end inspection (once in an hour/ need based whichever is earlier) and continuous monitoring of weights and defects and rectification of defects.

05. Effective handing overcharge of machine between the workmen during shift change and respective workstations.

06. The existing norms of production, quality assurance, housekeeping, responsible workmanship including daily shift duties and responsibilities, etc., remain unchanged.

VI. THE CALCULATION OF PLP FOR OTHER DEPTS

a) COLD-END—NORMS

80% of Forming PLP.

CRITICAL	MAJOR	MINOR	INCENTIVE AMOUNT
0%	1%	2–4%	80% of Forming PLP

01. Subject to material being of Minimum Acceptance Quality (MAQ) level, i.e., Critical Defect—0%, Major Defect—1%, and Minor Defect—2%–4%. If the material is not meeting MAQ, then no incentive will be given.

02. Thereafter, every 0.1% reduction in major defect from 1% level, sorter will get 0.50 paisa extra, and 0.5% reduction in minor defect, sorter will get Rs.1/– extra.

03. PWA may be performed by Cold End Quality Control Staff to determine the percentage heldware, if any.

04. The existing norms of production, quality assurance, housekeeping, responsible workmanship including daily shift duties and responsibilities, etc., remain unchanged.

b) FOUNDRY NORMS:

80% of Forming PLP.

01. In the case of foundry, incentive will be based on targeted production. At present, workers are doing ten heats of cast iron and 9 heats of minox. If any heat is rejected, foundry will have disincentive on similar line with CNC.

02. Machine-wise and operation-wise normal output level to be maintained by the individual operators.

03. Operators should work for more than the normal level (regular production output level) for achieving the incentive.

04. Job card entries and inspection reports should be recorded.

05. Job numbering and identification to be maintained and continued.

06. Operators should own the responsibilities of quality of items produced. Should ensure the rejected items traceable with proper markings.

07. Shift start and end timings should be strictly maintained.

08. Operators should ensure proper cleaning and maintenance of their respective machine and machine area and workplace at the end of the each shift.

09. Operators are requested for proper cooperation for any developmental activities like TPM, change.

c). SANDPLANT—NORMS:

80% of Forming PLP.

10. Sand plant has to be operated in the most effective manner with minimum breakdown so as to obtain daily production as per the requirements. Daily target for a month/fortnight will be issued by the management. In case targeted production is not achieved, no incentive will be given.

11. The existing norms of production, quality assurance, housekeeping, responsible workmanship including daily shift duties and responsibilities, etc., remain unchanged.

IV. MAINTENANCE—NORMS:

78% of Forming PLP.

01. To be eligible for incentive, there has to be a certificate issued by the maintenance department confirming all preventive maintenance schedules, checks being carried out excluding plant shutdown. If production is affected any other breakdown either in compressors/blowers/Lehr or any other major equipments to that extent, pro rata reduction will be made from the eligible incentive scheme.

02. The existing norms of production, quality assurance, housekeeping, responsible workmanship including daily shift duties and responsibilities, etc., remain unchanged.

V. FURNACE AND BATCH HOUSE

82% of Forming PLP.

01. Operators of furnace and Batch House and all other technicians will have to ensure that all furnace parameters/temperature/furnace level/ optimisation are duly taken care of. If due to any shutdown/breakdown excluding plant shutdown, the operation of the furnace affected resulting into loss of production, pro rata reduction will be made.

02. The existing norms of production, quality assurance, housekeeping, responsible workmanship including daily shift duties and responsibilities, etc., remain unchanged.

PLP FOR INDIVIDUAL DEPARTMENT—
ACL AND MOULD SHOP(CNC)

PERFORMANCE-LINKED PAY (PLP)			
MACHINE	PRODN/DAY	MAX.PRODN	AT SPEEDS
4 CLS 200	205,000	259,200	180
4 CS 125	95,000	144,000	100
2 CS 125	90,000	144,000	100

PLP CALCULATION			
Rupees	Production in nos. per day		
	4 CLS 200	4 CS 125	2 CS 125
225	205,000	95,000	90,000
275	220,000	105,000	100,000
325	230,000	115,000	105,000
375	240,000	120,000	110,000
425	250,000	125,000	115,000
475	260,000	130,000	120,000
525	270,000	135,000	125,000
575	280,000	140,000	130,000
625	290,000	145,000	135,000

Terms and Conditions:

01. General terms and conditions remain same as per the glass plant.

   a) If the employees are on deputation in other departments, they will get incentive as per their respective areas of work at the point of time.

   b) Water wash rejection should be maintained within 6%. If it exceeds, no incentive will be paid.

   c) Production quantities shown above are packed quantity and confirming to quality standards.

   d) The existing norms of production, quality assurance, housekeeping, responsible workmanship including daily shift duties and responsibilities, etc., remain unchanged

VI. MOULD SHOP (CNC)

MOULD SHOP—PERFORMANCE LINKED PAY (PLP)	
PRODUCTION IN CAVITIES	**PLP AMOUNT/RS**
330	200
350	240
370	280
380	320
390	375
410	425
420	475
430	525
440	575
450	650
460	775
470	825

01. REQUIREMENTS OF MOULD SHOP AND FOUNDRY

a) Machinewise and operationwise normal output level to be maintained by the individual operators.

b) Operators should work for more than the normal level (regular production output level) for achieving the incentive.

c) Job card entries and inspection reports should be recorded.

d) Job numbering and identification to be maintained and continued.

e) Operators should own the responsibilities of quality of items produced. Should ensure the rejected items traceable with proper markings.

f) Shift start and end timings should be strictly maintained.

g) Operators should ensure proper cleaning and maintenance of their respective machine and machine area and workplace at the end of the each shift.

h) Operators are requested for proper cooperation for any developmental activities like TPM, change.

i) The below mentioned table is used to arrive at weightage for incentive calculation in respect of various jobs being executed in Mould Shop.

WEIGHTAGE FOR INCENTIVE CALCULATION	
	Weightage
Up to 70 mL	0.7
71–100 mL	0.9
101–200 mL	1.0
201–750 mL	1.2
751 mL and above	1.5

NECK RING–CAVITY CONVERSION RATIO = 3:

IX—NATIONAL AND FESTIVAL HOLIDAYS

01. The National and Festival Holidays will be twelve days in a calendar year as per the existing practice.

02. It is agreed by and between the parties that employees who are all working in regular shift on any National and Festival Holidays declared in Form No. V of the National and Festival Holidays Act one-day wages for National and Festival Holidays plus double

wages working on National and Festival Holiday or one-day wages for working on National Festival Holiday plus one wage plus one-day compensatory off. Based on the exigency of the work and the nature of our continuous process industry, the alternative choice of claiming compensatory off will be allowed at the discretion of the management.

03. In case any workman is required to attend duties on a weekly off which falls on the National and Festival holiday, the concerned workman shall be entitled for one-day wages for National and Festival Holiday plus thrice the wages or twice the wages along with one-day compensatory off will be paid.

04. If the weekly off happens to be on any of the National and Festival Holidays, the concerned workmen will be entitled for either one-day additional wage for National and Festival Holiday apart from weekly off or compensatory off in lieu of additional wage for National and Festival Holiday apart from weekly off.

05. The compensatory off occurred as per clause no. 02, 03, and 04, the concerned workman shall have to avail the compensatory off within sixty days.

X—ANNUAL INCREMENT

01. It is agreed by both the parties that the annual increments will be granted as per the existing increment scale as detailed below on the first of April every year to the confirmed workmen.

		A	B	C	D
Band I	Unskilled, semi-skilled I, and semi-skilled II	45	35	25	0
Band II	Skilled I, skilled II, skilled III	50	40	30	0
Band III	Highly skilled I, highly skilled II	60	50	40	0

02. It is agreed that the rating will be based on Annual Performance Appraisal done by the management every year and the decision of the management with regard to rating and increment shall be final and binding to all the workmen. The annual increment as decided by the management will be added to the basic salary drawn by the individual workmen.

03. It is expressly agreed by and between the parties that a workman who will not put in physical attendance of 240 days in a year will not be entitled for annual increment.

04. It is mutually agreed that annual increment for the year 2006–07 shall be disbursed effective Sept '06. Administrative delays if any shall be condoned by the workmen and the union.

XI—PROMOTION

01. Promotion is the sole discretion of the management and cannot be claimed as a matter of right. The workman shall be given promotion without discrimination and with due regard to his work

efficiency, initiative, discipline, positive attitude, willingness to take additional responsibility, learning attitude, team building skill, achievement of results, and job requirement

XII—WAGES AND ADVANCES

01. It is agreed that the standard rate of monthly wages means the sum of Basic + VDA + HRA + Conveyance Allowance + Washing Allowance + LTA + Education Allowance + Medical Allowance only.

02. It is agreed that month means twenty-six days.

03. It is agreed that one-day wages means standard rate of monthly wages divided by twenty-six days.

04. It is agreed by both the parties that the workman who absent without approval or absent without pay or leave without pay up to ten days in a month, the present practice of calculating loss of pay by deducting Basic + VDA + Conveyance + Washing Allowance will continue and for the purpose of deduction, the divisor will be twenty-six.

05. Both the parties agreed that any workmen who absent without approval or absent without pay or leave without pay for more than ten days in a month, the workman shall not be eligible for any wages during the said period and for the purpose of deduction, the divisor will be twenty-six.

06. The net pay including allowances, after all deductions, that is payable to every workman will be rounded off to the nearest one rupee. For the purpose of payment, fifty paisa and more will be rounded off to rupee one and less than fifty paisa will be ignored.

07. The present practice of payment of monthly wages by directly crediting to the bank account of the workmen will continue.

08. It is agreed that for calculating overtime payment, the existing practice to sum up Basic + VDA will be divided by twenty-six and then divided by eight shall continue.

09. Both parties agreed that there will not be any salary/ wage advance during the period of this settlement as per the existing practice.

10. Both parties agree that there will not be any festival advance during the period of this settlement as per the existing practice.

XIII—CANTEEN

01. The company will continue to provide the canteen facility through an outside contractor.

02. Canteen shall be opened only during the scheduled time.

	Shift	Time—Hours
Breakfast	First (A)	0530 to 0555
Breakfast	General (G)	0730 to 0755
Lunch	First (A)	1000 to 1100
Lunch	General (G)	1200 to 1300
Dinner	Second (B) shift	1900 to 2000
Breakfast	Third (C)	0200 to 0300

03. It is agreed by both parties that if there is any increase in the price of canteen food items, it will be revised once in *three* months on the basis of three months average cost.

04. The average cost for the month of October, November, and December will be the basis for computing the revised rate for January, February, and March every year. The quarterly basis approach shall be applied for rest of the months in a given period of one year.

05. At present, the management is incurring *Rs. 351/–* towards canteen subsidy per employee per month. Any increase over and above the existing subsidy being borne by the management, it is specifically agreed by both the parties that the same will be shared at *50:50* ratio between the management and employees.

The basis for cost calculation is as follows:

	May-05	Jun-05	Jul-05	Average	Comp. Contribution	Amount
Tea	16,708	15,782	12,928	15,139	1.05	15,896
Breakfast	2,833	2,873	2,751	2,819	1.60	4,510
Lunch	4,822	4,522	4,493	4,612	5.25	24,215

Service charge	36,000	36,000	36,000	36,000		36,000
LPG	40,000	40,000	40,000	40,000		40,000
Total						120,621
Emp	344	344	344	344		344

Total amount divided by average
no. of employees = Rs.351

Illustration

Assuming that if the cost incurred by the management is Rs 400/– per employee per month, the amount over and above Rs 351/– i.e. Rs. 49/– shall be shared by both parties at employees Rs. 24.50/per month and the management Rs. 24.50/– per employee per month.

The increased amount of Rs.24.50/– will be apportioned on the following basis as per the supplementary guidelines enclosed in the *Annexure 'B'*.

24.50 × 67% divided by 18 = Rs. 0.91—will be added to each Lunch Coupon.
24.50 × 25% divided by 17 = Rs.0.36—will be added to each Tiffin Coupon.
24.50 × 8% divided by 52 = Rs.0.04—will be added to each Tea Coupon

Hence the revised rate of items will be as follows:

ITEM	Present Rate Per Item Coupon (Rs)	50% Share Per Item Coupon (Rs)	Revised Rate Per item Coupon (Rs)
Tea	0.25	0.04	0.29
Tiffin	3.00	0.36	3.36
Meals	7.00	0.91	7.91

06. The union/workmen further specifically agreed the following norms of conduct and practices in the canteen.

a. No workmen shall be allowed to take canteen food items for any reason outside the factory.

b. Any two office bearers of the union will be included along with management representatives in determining price revision of canteen food items as per the above agreed norms.

c. Those workmen who are bringing own food items shall not be allowed to consume the same at any other premises in the company except the canteen.

d. Workmen shall strictly adhere to self-service systems in the canteen.

e. Workmen shall remove used plates/dishes and place them at the disposal counter earmarked for the purpose.

f. All the workmen shall wash their hands in the designated washbasin only.

g. Workmen shall not wash their hands over the used plates or other dishes or down the table inside the dining hall.

h. At any point of time maximum of two Canteen Committee members shall only be allowed to enter the kitchen for inspection purpose.

i. All other workmen are strictly prohibited to enter the canteen kitchen.

j. Workmen shall not throw any leftover food items on the floor of the canteen/company or in the washbasin.

k. Tea and biscuits will be served at tea points only.

l. Biscuits will not be supplied in packets in return for bunch of coupons.

m. The existing system of Overtime Coupon issued by the respective departments stands withdrawn with immediate effect.

n. Those workmen who are required to work overtime, the cost of the coupon borne by the workmen will be credited in their wages as per the following details:

- Minimum 2 but less than 4 hours OT —Cost of one tea only
- 4 hours only —Cost of one tea + One lunch
- 5.30 hours and up to 8 hours —Cost of two tea + One lunch

o. Workmen shall maintain strict discipline in the canteen and shall not argue with the Canteen Contractor on any matter. A workman having any grievances may approach the Administration Department. The administrative department will look into the grievance for required remedial action.

p. For all workmen, those who are taking food items shall have to give the coupon first to the canteen counter. Without coupon, food items will not be served under any circumstances.

XIV—TRANSPORT

01. It is agreed by and between the parties that employees utilising the transport facility provided by the management would be on payment basis. It

is agreed by both parties that the existing rate shall be revised once in *three* months.

02. Both parties agreed to revise the present rate if there is any increase. The average cost for the month of October, November, and December will be the basis for computing the revised rate for January, February, and March every year. The quarterly basis approach shall be applied for the rest of the months in a given period of one year.

03. At present, the management is incurring Rs.571/– per employee per month. Over and above the present cost, the increased amount shall be shared by both the management and employees at 50%:50% ratio.

The basis for cost calculation is as follows:

	May-05	Jun-05	Jul-05	Average
Bus	64,730	65,487	69,032	66,416
Mazda—32	46,777	49,595	50,217	48,863
Mazda—40	35,788	36,076	37,548	36,471
Total	147,295	151,158	156,797	151,750
(-) 218 Emp. Cont	27,250	27,250	27,250	27,250
Cost to the company	120,045	123,908	129,547	124,500
CTC/per head for 218 employees	551	568	594	571

Total amount divided by average no.
of. employees = Rs.571/–.

Illustration

Assuming that if the cost incurred by the management is Rs 590/– per employee per month. The amount over and above Rs 571/–, i.e., Rs.19/–, shall be shared by both parties

at employees Rs.9.50/– per month and the management
Rs.9.50/–per employee per month

04. The union/workmen further specifically agrees to
it as follows:

a) Any workmen travelling without valid bus pass
has to pay double the rate of monthly individual
share.

b) Monthly bus fare shall be deducted from the
wages of all workmen availing the bus service
irrespective of their attendance during the
month.

c) There shall be no demand for the conveyance
facility to be extended to any other route,
destination, pickup/drop points or for change
in the route. The existing departure schedule
shall remain unaltered.

d) The supplementary guidelines to arrive at
conveyance cost is enclosed in the *Annexure 'C'.*

XV—RAIN COAT/CAP

01. It is agreed by both the parties that the present
practice of issuing one rain coat once in two years
and issuing of one cap every year stands withdrawn
and abolished w.e.f. 01.09.2006. The equivalent
amount of Rs.597/– (Rs 497/– plus Rs 50/– * 2 caps)
(rupees five hundred and ninety-seven only) shall
be credited in the salary account of all permanent
workmen during January in the alternate years.
Next issue falls due only January 2007.

XVI—UNIFORM

01. It is agreed by both the parties that all the workmen shall be issued uniform once in a calendar year during January as per the existing practice. It is agreed that the management will pay Rs.150/– towards stitching charges of each set of uniform (Pant + Shirt).

02. The uniform will be stitched by strictly adhering to the stitching norms given by the management for this purpose. If the uniform is stitched not as per the specifications given by the management, the concerned workman shall not be allowed to work inside by wearing the unmatched uniform. The union should extend necessary cooperation in this regard to the management.

03. It is also agreed by the parties that the new practice of stitching allowance disbursement shall be reviewed by the management in January 2008 and appropriate decision regarding the continuance or otherwise of stitching allowance disbursement shall be taken. There after recurrence of deviation if any is found, the new system of issuing the uniform cloth and stitching charges will be withdrawn at any point of time. The management decision in this regard is final.

04. It is agreed that the management will issue uniform cloth to all workmen as per existing measurement scale enclosed in the *Annexure 'D'*.

XVII—GRATUITY

01. The workmen will be paid gratuity as per the provisions of the Payment of Gratuity Act, 1972. Both the parties specifically agreed that the Gratuity Service period shall not be affected by number of days lost due to the suspension of operation.

XVIII—GENERAL TERMS AND CONDITIONS

01. The workmen and the union specifically agree that they shall fully cooperate in such a manner so as not to disrupt the operations of the factory during the period of this settlement by resorting to any agitation, strike, or slow down of normal output and in any case without giving advance notice in writing to the management of at least fourteen days before resorting to any action along with a copy to the conciliation officer concerned.

02. The age of retirement or superannuation shall be on attaining 58 (fifty-eight) years.

XIX—LEAVE

01. The existing system of Leave Year is changed from Financial Year to calendar year with effect from the date of signing this settlement.

02. All permanent workmen shall be eligible for ten days' casual leave in a calendar year.

03. Casual leave shall be limited to 2 (two) days at a time.

04. Casual Leave shall not be claimed as a matter of right. It should be applied for sanction at least three days before commencement of the leave.

05. The unavailed portion of Casual Leave during the calendar year will not be carried forward to the next year.

06. All permanent workmen will be eligible for seven days' sick leave in a calendar year.

07. Any leave application for more than three days on ground of sickness shall be accompanied by a medical certificate issued by a registered medical practitioner.

08. All permanent workmen shall be eligible for privilege leave as per the following:

   a) All workmen who have worked for 240 days in the preceding calendar year shall be eligible for privilege leave at the rate of one day for every twenty days worked.

   b) The above period of 240 days shall be calculated by including number of days actually present, National and Festival Holidays, CL availed, sick leave availed, and privilege leave availed in the preceding calendar year.

   c) In case any workman has not worked 240 days in the preceding calendar year as per the above calculation, he will not be entitled for any privilege leave.

d) It is agreed by and between the parties that workmen shall be entitled for privilege leave during the year 2005–06 and 2006–07 on pro rata physical presence. This has been agreed by the management as a good will gesture irrespective of minimum requirement of 240 days as per the Factories Act.

09. Minimum privilege leave balance to be maintained for the encashment of PL is thirty days in a given period of time.

10. PL encashment is calculated by applying the following formula:

PL encashment = Basic + VDA / 26 * encashable days.

11. Workmen shall be allowed to avail privilege leave only for 3 (three) times in a calendar year.

12. Application for privilege leave should be submitted at least ten days before the commencement of leave except in the case of unforeseen situations.

13. The grant of privilege leave shall be the prerogative of the management.

14. No leave shall be admissible to a workman who is under suspension.

15. The workmen shall be prohibited in availing any leave during the ESI leave period.

16. All National and Festival Holiday including weekly off falling within the period of any kind of leave shall not be treated (counted) as part of leave.

XX—BONUS

01. It is agreed that bonus for the financial year April 2005 to March 2006 will be paid on pro rata at 8.33% to all the eligible workmen as per the Payment of Bonus Act, 1965.

02. It is further agreed that in addition to the above bonus, an ex-gratia amount of Rs. 2,916/– (two thousand nine hundred and sixteen only) shall be admissible, upon fulfilling the following two conditions:

   ✓ The workman should have worked during the financial year April 2005 to March 2006.

   ✓ The workman shall be on live rolls of the company as on 01.10.2006.

a. It is also agreed that all workmen who are not eligible for bonus as per the Payment of Bonus Act will be paid Rs. 4,999/– as ex gratia upon fulfilling the following three conditions.

   ✓ The workman should have worked during the financial year April 2005 to March 2006.

   ✓ The workman shall be on live rolls of the company as on 01.10.2006.

b.   The union and workmen agreed not to raise or pursue any demand relating to the payment of bonus for the said financial year before any forum whatever at any point of time in future.

c.   It is also agreed that bonus and ex gratia payment shall be made on pro rata basis to the workmen for the financial year April 2006 to March 2007.

XXI—GOODWILL GESTURE

01. The union requested that since they have agreed that no settlement benefits are to be extended to them for the period from 01.07.2005 to 25.01.2006, the management might, however, consider some payment by way of goodwill gesture keeping in mind the harmonious relations between the parties.

02. The management agreed that all workmen who are on rolls of the company as of 01.07.2005 and continue to be on the rolls of the company before the expiry of ten days from the date of signing this settlement will be paid a goodwill gesture amount of Rs. 6,700/– (rupees six thousand seven hundred only) as onetime payment.

03. The union and workmen agreed that they will not raise any demand directly or through any union whatsoever involving any direct or indirect financial burden of any nature on the company for the period from 01.07.2005 to 25.01.2006.

XXII—WITHDRAWAL OF PENDING DISPUTES

01. In view of this 12(3) settlement, it is agreed that union shall withdraw the following cases on or before 30th September 2006 pending for disposal as the respective issues are duly addressed through mutual agreement between the management and the union.

   - ✓ No. .... dated 03.10.2005 regarding Changes of Service Conditions under Section 9A of the Industrial Dispute Act 1947, and failure report thereof before the conciliation machinery.
   - ✓ .... pending on the file of Deputy Commissioner of Labour-cum-conciliation officer regarding payment of wages dispute.
   - ✓ .... of 2005 pending before the Hon'ble High Court, regarding Writ of MANDAMUS restraining the management not to implement change of service conditions.
   - ✓ WPMP. No. .... in WP No. .... of 2005 pending before the Hon'ble High Court, regarding Writ of MANDAMUS directing the management to discontinue with suspension of operation.

XXIII—SUSPENSION OF OPERATION

01. Whereas the go-slow strike/intermittent strike and acts of indiscipline took place during December 2005 and January 2006, the management had no

option but to declare suspension of operation on 25.01.2006 for the safety and security of personnel and the plant in the prevailing circumstances.

02. Since the go-slow strike led to the suspension of operations by the management to avert imminent the crisis situation, which might lead to safety and fire hazards. The Labour Commissioner in his capacity as conciliation officer intervened in the dispute for reaching amicable settlement between the parties. Subsequently, the parties to the dispute after having a series of discussion arrived at mutual settlement in the form of 12(3) settlement as per the Industrial Disputes Act 1947. The Labour Commissioner requested the management to lift the suspension of operations for resumption of production activities in the plant.

03. Since there was no production from 25.01.2006 to 31.08.2006, union and workmen specifically agreed that they shall not be entitled for any wages or monetary benefits for the said period on the basis of 'No Work No Pay' principle.

04. The management and the workmen mutually agreed to restore normal production activities in the plant based on improved productivity, total quality, cost reduction, waste reduction, and customer satisfaction.

05. The workmen and the union agreed to cooperate with the company in its efforts to make continuous improvement in the areas of new technology

adaptation, modernisation of machines, and rationalisation of plant operation by way of changing/removing required and obsolete machines/equipment and installing new machines/equipments as well as whenever and wherever deems it appropriate to implement changes in the methods, processes, and systems not withstanding any express or implied dispute in this regard.

XXIV—PERIOD OF VALIDITY

01. This settlement shall come into effect from 01.09.2006 and it shall remain in force for a period of four years, i.e., up to 31.08.2010. It shall remain in force thereafter unless terminated by either party according to the provisions of Industrial Disputes Act 1947.

Dated at .... on .... September Two Thousand Six

Representatives MANAGEMENT   Representatives WORKMEN

ANNEXURE B—
SUPPLEMENTARY GUIDELINES—CANTEEN

a) Food items per head calculation:

Assume that one employee's total attendance is twenty-six days, A shift nine days, B shift nine days, and C shift eight days. Then, the canteen facility avails by him will be as follows:

A shift 9 days (Lunch + BF)	=	9 Lunches + 9 BF
B shift 9 days (Lunch	=	9 Lunches
C shift 8 days (BF)	=	8 BFs
Tea (26 × 2)	=	52 Nos.

Hence one workman will be having 18 Lunches, 17 BF, and 52 Tea during one month of normal attendance.

b) Proportionate cost of food items: -

Cost of Lunch	=	Rs. 12.25
Cost of BF	=	Rs. 04.60
Cost of Tea	=	Rs. 01.30
Total	=	Rs. 18.15

Percentage of other cost to be added to food items:

Lunch	Rs. 12.25 divided by 18.15	=	67.49% or 67%
BF	Rs. 04.60 divided by 18.15	=	25.34% or 25%
Tea	Rs. 01.30 divided by 18.15	=	07.1

ANNEXURE C—
SUPPLEMENTARY GUIDELINES—TRANSPORT

TRANSPORT RATES (w.e.f. 06-06-06) AND INCREASE

PRESENT RATE	Rs.15.34 per K.M.
CONSUMPTION	3 km/L
INCREASE	Inc. Amount / 3 + Current Rate
DECREASE	Dec. Amount / 3 – Current Rate
Current rate – Inc. Amt / 3	
Current Rate – Dec. Amount / 3	
Working	
Diesel rate as on 06.06.06	Rs.33.80
Diesel rate as on 07.09.05	Rs.31.72
Amount increase	Rs.2.08
Per km increase (2.08/3)	Rs.0.69
Rate w.e.f. 06.06.06 (14.65 + 0.69)	Rs.15.34

Note: Consumption was 6 km/L and was amended to 3 km/L w.e.f. 01 July 2004 on 09.03.2005 with retrospective effect.

MAZDA 32 SEATER (PY 01 N 4648)

PRESENT RATE	Rs.10.39 per K.M.
CONSUMPTION	6 km/L.
INCREASE	Inc. Amount / 6 + Current Rate
DECREASE	Dec. Amount / 6 – Current Rate

Working	
Diesel rate as on 06.06.06	Rs.33.80
Diesel rate as on 07.09.05	Rs.31.72
Amount increase	Rs.2.08
Per km increase (2.08/3)	Rs.0.35
Rate w.e.f. 06.06.06 (14.65 + 0.69)	Rs.10.39

MAZDA 40 SEATER (PY 01 × 8786)

Driver Charges	Rs. 6,000/– p.m.
Maint. Charges	Rs. 4,500/– p.m.
Service Charges	Rs. 3,000/– p.m.

Running Charges	Total km run × Rs.5.63
	(rate per km)
Consumption	6 km/L
Current Rate (1 L cost /)	Rs.5.63/km

ANNEXURE D—
MEASUREMENT SCALE—UNIFORM (TECHNICAL)

S. No.	DEPARTMENT	NO. OF SETS		TC		COTTON	
		TC	COTTON	SHIRT	PANTS	SHIRT	PANTS
1	Mould Shop	3	0	2.4 MTS	1.3 MTS*	2.5 MTS	2.5 MTS
2	Foundry	2	2				
3	BH/FUR	2	1	*Pants double breadth			
4	Machine Maintenance	2	2				
5	Forming	2	2				
6	ACL	3	0				
7	Mechanical	3	0				
8	Electrical	3	0				
9	Instrumentation	3	0				
10	Sand Plant	3	0				
11	Mould Repair	3	0				
12	Cold End Maintenance	3	0				
13	Cold End QC	3	0				
14	Customer Support	3	0				
15	Quality Assurance	3	0				
16	Design	3	0				

MEASUREMENT SCALE—
UNIFORM (NONTECHNICAL)

SN	*DEPT*		TC	*TC*	
				SHIRT	PANT
1	Accounts	2	2.4 MTS	1.3 MTS*	
2	Commercial	2			
3	Systems	2			
4	HR	2			
5	Stores	2			
6	Warehouse	2			
7	VP	2			

Note: i) Three sets of uniform will be given to new joiners.
ii) *Pants double breadth

Conclusion | 8

Conclusion: Hard Leads to Soft or Soft Leads to Hard

Essence of Human Resources Management has laid down basic governing principles in dealing with people and their association in the form of unions. One such governing principle is fairness in accommodating their views instead of remaining strangely sided with business administration.

Today's managements seem to be taking a 'Hard' and 'Business Like' view at the expense of softer championship, advocacy, and people connect dimensions. Narrowing of relationship is creating unprecedented adjustment and consequences in terms of interruptions in smooth running of industries. Unfortunately, slew of Indian organisations which originally had a broader relationship with employees are inadvertently moving the other way and that does not seem like a great idea. On account of dynamic business environment infused by VUCA world, such kind of HARD stand of the management might force the employees or the union to adopt conciliatory gestures for short-term period but eventually feelings erupt at certain times in the form of direct action where the management may be caught completely unaware.

It may be counterintuitive to argue that employees or the union may take SOFT approach of the management for granted. To be very precise, Human Relations approach is placed on premium vis-à-vis economic exchange relationship. Research findings or experiences might prove to be either 'for' or 'against' this point of view. Sometimes, SOFT approach could fail to communicate business exigencies in the right perspective to the people in large numbers in managing workplace conflicts as a reaction to the HARD stand being adopted by the employees or the Union. Then HARD approach of the management may soften the muscle flexing attitude of the employees or the union.

Nevertheless, Human Relations exchange approach based on the feelings of a large number of people, if shapes the management philosophy in managing workplace relationship, then there is going to be a paradigm shift in the employees to have cautious optimism in constructively addressing their grievances or disputes on long-term basis.

To succinctly put in, both Push (HARD) and Pull (SOFT) strategies are being deployed in managing both existing or emerging workplace relationship issues depending upon various situations. Sometimes the HARD stand of the management or employees/union might proves to be effective in subordinating each others' expectations to the ground realities. If SOFT stand is being taken by both the parties, not as a reaction to the crisis but as a philosophy in managing each other's expectations as a governing principle, then over a period of time, it will lead to establishment of what is known as 'Mutual Investment Employment Relationship' towards healthy Employee Relationship. Hopefully, this deep-rooted SOFT approach may not give any chance for either of the parties to introspect and switch over to HARD stand later.

Probably the below mentioned four factors bring in long-term harmony between HARD and SOFT approaches being resorted to either by the management or the employees/union.

1. **CONSTRUCTIVE PREOCCUPATION BETWEEN STRATEGIC PARTNER AND CHAMPIONING PEOPLE WELFARE**

HR needs to balance business interests with that of peoples' interests. Both are mutually inclusive. Likewise, the employees/union needs to appreciate business challenges while advocating strongly for employee welfare.

2. **RECIPROCAL EXISTENCE**

Soft approach of the management or HR may meet with fair amount of reciprocity from the employees. Using the depth of relationship, HR will be able to quickly resolve sticky people issues, negotiate with the union representatives, and hire/retain employees. Likewise, the constructive approach of the union need not be misinterpreted by the management in the light of weak bargaining position.

3. **FACILITATIVE ORGANISATIONAL DESIGN**

Organisation scale never before is up in direction feverishly. HR presence becomes meaningless if it needs to spread beyond certain limit. HR needs to organise itself into myriad of subverticals such as TA, Talent Engagement, Talent Development, Employee Relations, etc., leading to efficiency within the department with respect to not only a portfolio but rather holographic view of HR function or the whole human being. Probably, HR can take a leadership position to facilitate Organisational Redesign from the viewpoint of timely decision-making process and its execution thereof. Likewise, there must be a respect for union leadership or union structure for orderly transaction of business based on fairness and human welfare.

4. MORE SCIENCE/ART AND LESS TECHNIQUES/PROCESSES

Understanding of human behaviour and their motives come first in the list rather than getting overwhelmed by certain techniques/processes such as Talent Engagement or competency assessment or development. For shop floor community, the abovementioned conference room jargons or boardroom communication nuances do not make any impact or influence. In my personal opinion, still they are concerned about basic level needs such as better canteen facilities, better amenities such as good transportation, safe and secure work systems, better shop floor workplace relationship, education and health needs of their family members, etc. This approach will certainly permeate empathy and caring down the line leading to less workplace relationship issues.

Like keeping pace with constructive confrontation, union leadership should also promote transparency and skill development for the benefit of their rank and file.

Exhibits

Business IR Interface

Glossary of Terms Used

Major concepts used in the book are explained in operational terms by clubbing the theoretical definition from various sources and the context in which these concepts are used.

9A PROVISIONS (ID ACT 1947)	Certain rules governing change of working conditions to be observed by the employers having direct bearing on workmen.
12-3 SETTLEMENT (ID ACT)	Parties to the disputes settle their bilateral differences through the officer appointed constitutionally by the government.
BUSINESS SYNERGY	An ecosystem in the business entity in which it can successfully integrate various subsystems or functions to a common goal.
CLOSURE	Closing the place of industrial establishment including its legal entity.
CONCILIATION	A process whereby senior officials of labour dept enable both the parties to the dispute in arriving at mutual settlement through the art of persuasion and negotiation.
CONFLICT	When two or more parties in the given situation look at the issues from a different perspectives than on a common perspective which eventually results in either of the parties determined to object the other through deviant behaviours.
DIRECT ACTION	Pressure tactics being adopted by either the management or the union in order to achieve their goals or demands.

DISCHARGE SIMPLICITER	It is a condition of nonemployment infused by the management with respect to workmen that their behaviour or grave misconduct does not warrant any more tolerance or waiting time in taking befitting disciplinary action to protect the business interest for the sake of common good.
EMPLOYEE RELATIONS	Quality of relationship existing directly between the management and individual employees based on co-partnership philosophy.
GHERAO	Serious misconduct on the part of employees whereby they physically block the human target even from attending to basic biological needs.
GO-SLOW AGITATION	One form of direct action by the workmen wherein they carry out assigned work less than the normal speed or efficiency.
HR LEADERSHIP	An individual in charge of Human Resources functions who takes decisions based on what is right and fair to promote the business interests as well as genuine people interests.
INDUSTRIAL RELATIONS	Collective relationship existing between the management and the employees or their unions in maintaining industrial peace for mutual benefits.
INJUNCTION	Legal remedy received by the aggrieved party against the opponent by restraining the latter to continue or initiate the purported action to the perceived or actual detriment of the latter.
LAYOFF	The failure, refusal, or inability of an employer to give employment to a workman on account of reasons directly connected with commercial or business aspects other than retrenchment.
LEADERSHIP INTEGRITY	Ability of an executive to lead the business and its people with zero tolerance on ethical or behavioural values being followed.
LINE LEADERSHIP	Senior level executives who are engaged with all technical functions beginning with production through delivery.

PERFORMANCE LINKED PAY	Method of compensation based on the number of units or quantity produced by the labour which aims at achieving business edge and shop floor motivation.
PRODUCTIVITY	It is a measure of efficiency which is determined based on input–output ratio.
SETTLEMENT	Final determination of an industrial dispute through mutual negotiation or being facilitated by an authority stipulated under relevant legislations.
SUSPENSION OF PLANT OPERATIONS	Closing the plant operations either partially or wholly on account of reasons attributed by troubled industrial relations situations.
UNION	Association of employees who subscribe to certain charter of undertaking and leadership being provided by either political parties or an independent body.

About the Author

An HR professional with more than twenty-three years of live-wire experience in HRM, Industrial Relations, Strategic Management, Quality Management System, Labour Welfare, and General Administration, Dr K. Suresh Kumar believes that professional commitment and contributions can be enriched through continuous learning.

Having done Postgraduate Programmes in Personnel Management, HRM, Training and Development, he has acquired a doctorate degree (PhD) in Management from University of Kerala. The thesis subject was 'Career Growth and Success of Managerial Professionals'.

Dr Suresh Kumar is having professional experience with topnotch companies in India including Thapar, Somani, Nicholas Piramal, Dalmia, and Aurobindo Pharma Ltd. Besides, he possesses sound experience in IT and ITES companies. As a keen enthusiast in professional training and development activities, he has been on board with various Indian Universities and Public–Private Sector Organisations to handle HR programmes. He has designed five management CDs and published more than 27 articles in various management journals apart from authoring the widely acclaimed management bestseller 'HR Can Win' in collaboration with Excel Books, New Delhi.

He has also won 'Young Manger's Trophy' for outstanding contribution towards modern HR Practices from NIPM.

Printed in the United States
By Bookmasters